CRUCIFY THE BASTARD

HOW TO COME OUT AHEAD IN YOUR DIVORCE

Jon M. Saltzman, Esq
with Elizabeth A. Jenkins, PhD

This is a work of nonfiction. However, the names and personal information of clients and judges have been changed in order to protect their identities. Any resemblance to actual people living or dead is entirely coincidental.

This book refers only to United States law, unless it specifically states otherwise.

Contents

Acknowledgments

Throughout the process of writing this book, I have been supported, inspired, and guided by so many friends, family, and clients, that I will inevitably fail to list everyone who has helped me bring this book to fruition. To all of you that played the valuable role of inspiring, conceptualizing, writing, editing, and/or publishing this book, I am incredibly grateful.

I am thankful to all my friends and family who have patiently listened to my ideas as this book took shape, and I would like to offer my specific thanks to Karen Nicholson and Elizabeth Jenkins for reviewing multiple drafts and always being willing to listen to my many stories.

I am grateful for Jason Wilcox whose willingness to share his immense knowledge and experience in publishing has been invaluable. Huge appreciation to Brent Underwood for sharing his wisdom in marketing books and helping this book to reach its intended audience.

A big thanks to all of my clients, but for you this book would not exist. I continue to wish you success and happiness as you move forward in your lives. To my children (Kira, Aaron, and Josh) and my "step-children" (Emily and Porter), you own my heart and are the reason that books like this are so important. I would also like to thank Robin. You could never be simply "my ex-wife," you are the mother of my children and you will always be my friend.

Lastly, I am and will always be thankful for my best friend and partner, Elizabeth Jenkins, who has not only contributed important chapters about the emotional aspects of divorce, she has also been a patient partner throughout the writing and editing process, and she continues to encourage and inspire me to be the best that I can be.

Introduction

Your lawyer is like your hired gun... but it is your job to provide the bullets. Given enough bullets, even a poor shot will eventually hit the target. Crucify the Bastard will arm you with information about how to support your lawyer so that you come out ahead in your divorce. You will learn how to create the bullets for every aspect of your divorce including custody, spousal and child support, property division and more.

*Your lawyer is like your hired gun...
but it is your job to provide the bullets.*

This book will also educate you about what you will likely face in a divorce, along with how you should prepare. Knowledge about the process will provide you with a huge advantage with the added benefit of eliminating your fear of the unknown.

Lastly, this book will give you, the reader, some insight into the behind the scenes thinking of the lawyers, judges, and other professionals with whom you will be working. The bottom line is that this book is a useful resource for anyone who is contemplating or already going through a divorce.

During the initial consultation with a new client, after gathering all the pertinent background information and before launching into my discussion and analysis of the case, I would routinely ask my client, "What are you hoping to have me achieve?" Two thirds of the women I saw responded with, "Crucify the bastard!" Those three words were my marching orders, and that is exactly what I did. The bottom line is that I not only did my job well, but I left my clients happy with the results.

My law firm grew and prospered because I consistently guided my clients through one of the most difficult and stressful periods of their lives and exceeded their expectations with the outcome. My recipe had three parts: inform and educate my client as to the likely results and make sure that her expectations were realistic; make my client my partner, so she always knew and understood our short-term and long-term goals each step of the way; and, most importantly, focus my client so that she could gather and provide me with the best ammunition possible. My clients understood that, while I was their "gun," they needed to provide me with the majority of the bullets. I simply taught them what kind of information I needed and how to gather it.

At least 70% of my clients were women and 90% of these women were angry. In this book, I will share my theories as to why and how they got to be so angry. I will explain how this anger can be productive if properly channeled by the right lawyer, how to find and hire the right lawyer, and, most importantly, what a woman needs to do to be her lawyer's partner.

The truth be told, at the end of their cases, most of my clients were neither angry nor did they feel that they had crucified their husbands (though many of their husbands might have disagreed). However, my clients did get what they were entitled to and often a lot more. More importantly, my clients finished their cases feeling optimistic, prepared, and excited to start a new chapter in their lives.

Sadly, I have met hundreds of women who, in their own experience of divorce, felt further traumatized by their own lawyers as well as the divorce process itself. It is my sincere hope that this book will give you the knowledge and tools to get through divorce and begin to find your path to happiness.

Now, for the legal disclaimer (You had to know that was coming): For the most part, divorce law, child custody law, and support laws are state, not federal laws. This means that each and every state has its own unique set of laws that apply to divorce cases in that state. Of course, there are many areas that are similar in every state, but there are many differences too. You will need to hire a lawyer who is licensed to practice law in your own state to represent you. This book is not intended to be a do it yourself guide. Instead, this book is intended to help you pick the best lawyer for your circumstances, give you a rough idea of what is important in your case, and help you understand how to communicate effectively with your lawyer by giving him or her the information really needed to get you the best results.

Finally, this book will give you some insight into the behind-the-scenes thinking of the lawyers, judges, and other professionals with whom divorcing clients will be dealing. The bottom line is that this book can be a useful resource for anyone who is contemplating or already going through a divorce. Competent divorce lawyers will appreciate the recommendations in this book and will likely recommend it to their clients. Your husband and his lawyer will hate this guide, as they will find it much more difficult to defeat a well-prepared client-attorney team.

1

Choosing the Right Lawyer

Trust the expert.
My client Jeff was a jet engine mechanic. As we walked together to the courthouse for his case, he kept telling me what strategies he thought I should use and what questions he thought I should ask. Finally, I looked at him and asked, "Jeff, do you have any jets that you are working on right now?" "Well, yes," he responded, "I have several." I winked and added, "I think I will come over there this afternoon to guide you on how best to make those repairs." His initial look of surprise was immediately followed by a smile.

The point is that you need to pick the right professional and then let them do their job. The key is to pick the right lawyer that will have the skill, knowledge, and experience to get the right information from you when they need it, and then to shift the problems from your shoulders onto theirs, letting them go out there and get you what you are entitled to.

You feel angry. You are hurt and confused. Your emotions are clouding your thinking. You feel betrayed, and you are scared. You feel like you have been kicked hard in the stomach and can't breathe. You just want to punch him in the face. You want to *Crucify the Bastard*.

Death of a loved one and divorce are the two most traumatic events that impact people's lives. The big difference is that we all know everyone will eventually die. It is a life event that we expect or at least acknowledge will eventually happen. Divorce is often more devastating in some ways, because even though it's common knowledge that about half of all marriages end in divorce, almost everyone gets married with the full belief that they will be in the half whose marriages succeed.

In my experience, women are often more optimistic than men, and, even when a marriage is sick, women are more likely to believe that the problems can and will be resolved and that all will be fine. It has also been my observation that men are more likely to be passive/aggressive, engaging in behaviors that serve to push the woman to "make the move" and take action to end the marriage, even if the woman would prefer to try to heal the relationship. Often, the result is a wife who is angry and vulnerable.

You are facing a decision that could easily impact the rest of your life. A divorce is on your horizon and you need a lawyer. The challenge is to find the right lawyer.

It goes without saying that you want your lawyer to know this area of the law. The most common mistake made by women who end up unhappy with the results of their cases is to assume that, just because an attorney has a law degree and is licensed to practice law, he or she can properly handle a divorce case. Would you go to your family doctor if you needed brain surgery? Of course not, you would look for the best brain surgeon you could find.

Divorce law is complex and does require a specialist with unique training and experience. Beyond that, you want a divorce lawyer who can fully appreciate that you are in pain and not at your emotional best. The divorce specialist must be a patient teacher who is able to translate legalese into normal English. The divorce attorney will need to help you provide him or her with the right information at the right time, so he or she will need to be adept at explaining just what information is needed and when it will be needed. The divorce lawyer must make sure that you understand how your case will probably end as well as each and every step that it will take to get to that end. You will also need a divorce attorney whom you can totally trust... as if your life depends on it... because it just might.

Even if you don't want a divorce or you are not ready for a divorce, if you know that there are problems in your marriage, it is critically important that, at the very least, you get an education. That is, find out what you would face in a divorce, what rights you have, what you should do and not do, how you should prepare, what it will cost, and, most importantly, the likely result given your circumstances and the state in which you live. When your marriage is sick or maybe even dying, you may feel like a person walking down the middle of a highway late at night. You must decide to cross over to one side for a divorce or cross over to the other side to try to save your marriage. Only you can make that decision but staying in the middle of that highway too long is mentally unhealthy and potentially risky. Looking over your shoulder while standing in the middle of the road and wondering if you are going to get run down by a semi-truck increases the risk that you will get hurt.

Having a divorce lawyer is simply a tool you will need should you decide (or if the decision is made for you by your spouse) to end the marriage. Maybe you will never use that tool for a divorce, but, if your marriage is sick, you need to learn what that tool can do for you, and the-sooner-the-better rule applies here. The financial investment in some initial consultations with divorce lawyers will bring you peace of mind regardless of where you stand. Knowledge is power, and, in this case, that knowledge might help you sleep a lot better at night.

Finally, it is worth noting that, in most jurisdictions, the lawyers you consult with cannot later represent your spouse, even if you don't use them. Work hard to find out who the best and most competent divorce lawyers are; once you choose and meet with one, you will have the added relief that this top gun can't work against you later.

Find Some Lawyers to Interview

You should have an initial consultation with at least three divorce lawyers before choosing one, so your first step is to do some legwork to determine who these three lawyers will be. Before you even start this quest, read and complete the General Marital Summary Sheet listed in Appendix A. This information will be needed by every competent divorce lawyer and having it ready in advance will leave more time at the initial consultation for the lawyer to begin discussing your case rather than just gathering information. Email the information to the lawyer before you meet and bring several copies with you to the consultation.

Now, let's get back to picking the three lawyers for the initial consultation. First and foremost, you do want a specialist. This means you only want to interview lawyers who limit their practice to family law (i.e., divorce, custody, and support). Remember, the man who flies a Cessna on the weekends and the man who flies a jet for Delta Airlines are both called "pilots," but there is a huge difference in their experience and ability to fly. That airline pilot has thousands of flying hours under his belt, has probably experienced everything that could go wrong, and is ready to deal with it. Before you consider making an appointment with any attorney, call their firm and ask if that attorney provides representation in any areas other than family law. If the answer is yes, generally you should cross them off your list. However, outside of cities and in more rural areas, attorneys may have to provide more diverse practices to survive. If this is the case, at least look for ones whose practice is, at a minimum, 50% or more family/divorce law.

Lawyers themselves would much rather be specialists in one

area of the law, because being truly expert in one area is just a whole lot easier than trying to be competent in many areas. The reason most lawyers are not specialists in one area of the law is that they don't have a strong enough reputation in that one area to make a living doing just one thing. The lawyer that can afford to specialize is usually one with two important achievements. This lawyer is one that is not only extremely knowledgeable in the specialty area but is also good enough to have satisfied enough former clients to build the reputation that supports limiting his or her practice. This is the person you want representing you.

One of the best ways to find your divorce specialist is to make a trip to your local courthouse and ask to speak to the clerk who logs in the divorce cases. Generally, you will find that they are not allowed to "recommend" specific lawyers, so don't ask them to do that. Instead, ask if they can give you the names of the five attorneys that file the most divorces in your county. Be persistent and ask the same question several ways if you can't get an answer. Ask the clerk if they can just name some lawyers who file lots and lots of divorces off the top of their head. I have even known women who were successful at getting good names because they just started crying in front of the clerk, saying that they were desperate and begging for a few names of lawyers who do a lot of this type of work. In many places, the divorce filings might even be available online. Do some research and see what names keep coming up over and over.

Another method is to get as many recommendations as possible from friends and acquaintances. Give the most weight to those who have actually gone through a divorce and been represented by the specific attorney they are recommending. You will be surprised to learn that many thought their spouse's lawyer was better than theirs. Get those names. Hairdressers are also a great source for this type of information, as they spend a lot of time chatting with their clients. Don't just ask your particular hairdresser; ask every one of them in the salon or ask your hair stylist to do this for you. I would recommend giving less weight to recommendations made by other professionals (doctors, realtors, etc.) unless they have personally used the lawyer they are recommending for a divorce. Often, they will refer you to a friend or acquaintance who happens to be a lawyer, because they think he or she is nice. Being "nice" is not high up on the list of required attributes of a good divorce attorney.

If you have any form of relationship with an attorney, reach out for a recommendation, but be sure to specify that you are looking for an attorney who does nothing but divorce, or, if you are in a more rural area, an attorney who does divorces as the majority of his or her practice. I had a client who told me that she had never used a lawyer in her life. When she decided that she needed to find an attorney, she went to her local courthouse to have lunch in the courthouse cafeteria. She had lunch there every single day for a week, and, while there, she approached lawyers at random, asking for recommendations about attorneys who specialize in divorces. Spotting the lawyers in the cafeteria is a lot easier than you think. Believe me, they will stand out.

Do some online research. See which names come up most often when you do some different searches. Once you have narrowed down your list using all the methods talked about here, do a search on the attorney and find out how long they have been in practice, if they practice other areas of the law, and what kind of reviews they have from former clients.

Finally, determine how big a "gun" you will need. Even within the firms that specialize in divorce law, you will find different levels of experience, competency, reputations, and costs. There is an old saying that is unfortunately not far from the truth, and it goes, "America has the best system of justice money can buy; those with the money get to buy the justice." That said, while the top guns will cost the most, you may not need the top gun, and, even if you do, there are some ways to find a lawyer that will be just as good as the top guns, but not as expensive. Additionally, in many jurisdictions, depending on the circumstances, you may even be able to get the court to order your spouse to pay for some or all of your attorney's fees.

America has the best system of justice money can buy.
Those with the money get to buy the justice.

❦

Divorce specialists will generally fall into one of three categories: (1) The sole practitioner working out of their own office or sharing office space with other sole practitioners, (2) The attorney in a small firm (often called boutique firms with fewer than 20 lawyers) working as the senior partner, junior partner, or associate. This small firm may be all divorce specialists or may have specialists devoted to many areas of law, and (3) The divorce specialist working in a larger firm (more than 20 lawyers and, in many cities, more than 50 or 100 lawyers) where there are specialists in many different fields of law.

My recommendation would be to go with a lawyer from the first two categories above. I believe that generally you will save some money this way. With respect to the divorce lawyers themselves, I would divide them into three categories: (1) Top guns, (2) Competent practitioners, and (3) Lawyers doing divorces because they need the money. Identifying which group they fall into and which one you need will be an important consideration.

The top guns are lawyers that are not only thoroughly competent, but they have also earned the strongest reputations among their clients and peers. They will often be the most expensive, but this is one of those cases where you get what you pay for. Most of the top guns will be the named partners in their law firms and often the founders of their law firms.

If the net worth of the marital estate (total value less all the debt equals the net worth) is more than a million dollars (higher in some affluent urban areas), you will need a top gun. If you think there is a high likelihood of a custody battle, you will want a top gun. If your spouse is self-employed and you suspect the tax returns do not reflect the actual income, you may need a top gun. Also, if your spouse has total control of the marital assets and/or you suspect he has hidden assets in anticipation of getting a divorce, you will probably need a top gun. If you or your spouse is in a high-income bracket, you will probably need a top gun. If you signed a premarital agreement (prenuptial agreement) that you no longer think is fair, you will need a top gun to challenge it.

Now, perhaps you don't fit into any of the areas specified above or you just can't afford a top gun. While a skilled divorce specialist is still critically important, you may do just as well with a specialist that is a junior partner or an associate of a top gun. This lawyer will still be far more knowledgeable than most general practitioners, and he or she will have the benefit of supervision from the top gun divorce lawyer.

The Initial Consultation

Assuming that you have done your homework, filled out the General Marital Summary Sheet in Appendix A, and picked out three or more divorce lawyers to meet with, it's time to talk about what you should look for at that meeting. A lawyer should have great communication skills, although many are just not that good at communicating with their clients. Most good divorce specialists will spend some time exploring your expectations to determine if they are realistic. This is important for two reasons. First, if your expectations are unrealistic and the lawyer does not "bring you back to earth," this is a recipe likely to end in disappointment. There have been several instances in which I refused to take on a client and when asked why, I explained that castration was not legal in our state and that it was my feeling that she would not be satisfied with any result short of castration. A good divorce lawyer will be far more concerned with his own reputation than the fees he could potentially make on any particular case. A client with unrealistic expectations will never be happy with the results of the case and will inevitably blame their lawyer.

A divorce specialist should be able to tell you the probable outcome with the understanding that there can never be any guarantees. The lawyer should be able to tell you the likely result with respect to property division and the amount of child support and spousal support or alimony you will probably receive. The only area of outcome that the lawyer may not be able to accurately predict is custody.

Being able to accurately predict the probable outcome of your case is a critical skill, primarily because more than 90% of all divorce cases will be resolved with an out-of-court settlement. The probable outcome if your case were to go to trial is an important "keystone." The lawyer's goal must be to resolve your case, getting you at least what you would get if the case were to go to trial. If your lawyer does not have an accurate grasp of the outcome, he or she will do an abysmal job when it comes time to settle the case. If your attorney asks for far more than the likely result, the opposing lawyer, knowing this, will just let the case go to trial, since there is little to lose by doing so and his client will likely do better at trial. In this scenario, you will spend a lot in unnecessary legal fees. Alternatively, without a good grasp of the likely outcome, your lawyer might advise you to settle for far less than you would get at trial, in which case you would end up holding the short end of the stick.

Many lawyers are hesitant to share with you their opinions about the most likely, final result for your case. Some are hesitant because they don't have enough experience in divorce law and are just not educated enough in the specialty. Other lawyers are hesitant because they don't want to look bad if the actual final result is a lot different than what they originally said. I believe that a good, experienced, divorce lawyer should be giving you a qualified opinion with respect to all your issues except custody. If the lawyer you are interviewing is hesitant or will not give you an opinion as to a likely result, I would suggest you look for a different lawyer.

When I first started working in divorce law, I was happy when the opposing lawyer was inexperienced and not a divorce specialist. I believed that his ignorance would work to my client's advantage. I quickly learned that these lawyers that lacked experience in divorce law more often than not had unrealistic expectations, so that I had no choice but to try the case. Yes, my clients did far better than the off target offers that had been put on the table, but it ended up costing my client more money than it needed to.

When educating my clients as to the probable outcome, I explain that 90% of the divorce cases end with a settlement and yet, most of the time, those settlements do not occur until the costly divorce proceedings have gone on for some time. My message to you is this: a couple may choose to (a) pay to educate their attorneys' children (by fighting against a settlement) or (b) keep their money and use it to educate their own children (by settling early). The truth is, the reason that most settlements do not occur until well into the expensive process is that one or both parties has unrealistic expectations as to what the settlement should be or that one or both parties has a great deal of anger that needs time to diminish.

Good, experienced, divorce specialists never want or need to drag out your case to earn more. These lawyers have good reputations and all the work they can handle. Most of the time, when I have encountered people who were dissatisfied with the results of their case, it was usually because they did not have an experienced divorce specialist representing them and the case ended up costing more than it should have.

Besides telling you the probable outcome of your case, the lawyer should also explain each step that you will go through to reach completion of your divorce (we call these procedural steps). Additionally, an experienced divorce specialist should be able to give you a price range for getting through each of those steps. This information regarding the probable financial costs should be at the lawyer's fingertips, but it is almost never shared unless the client requests it. The bottom line is that this is not the time to be shy. Ask your attorney about the costs.

However, you do need to understand that, at best, the lawyer will probably only be able to give you a range for each procedural step as the actual amount will often vary depending on the actions taken by the opposing side.

A good attorney should be able to clearly explain the steps he or she will take when it comes to custody, support, and property division. You should be able to walk out of his or her office understanding the steps that your case will go through with each of these areas. Finally, if you have special concerns in any of these areas, like physical abuse against you or the children, your spouse's mental health issues as it relates to custody decisions, your spouse's hidden or cash income when it comes to support, or the possibility of hidden assets, you should make them known to the lawyer and then listen carefully to their explanation as to how they will deal with these problems.

Picking the Right Lawyer

Once you have had initial consultations with at least three lawyers, you "should" have heard essentially the same information from all of them. If you find that one or more did not communicate as much information as the others, eliminate that lawyer from the running. All good lawyers should have good communication skills, but the best lawyers can use those skills not only with the judges and other lawyers, but also and even more importantly, in my opinion, with their own clients. The best lawyers are teachers at heart and this trait is important. You need to know what is going on in your case, you need to know what the goals are and what the challenges are at each step of the way, and you need to know what the likely outcome will be. There is nothing worse than not knowing what is going on in your case. Your imagination will run wild with unlikely scenarios that are far worse than what will probably happen. Even if the likely result is unfavorable to you or far from what you are hoping for, knowing the realities of the likely probabilities is far better than not knowing at all. Again, one of the most common complaints of people who were unhappy with the results of their divorce case was that they felt they were in the dark and blindsided. You want to pick a lawyer you can understand and who takes the time to communicate with you and keep you informed. With the right lawyer, you should leave your initial consultation with an understanding for how the law in your state will apply to your case. You should also leave with an understanding about what the plan of action would be for your case and a rough idea as to what it would cost you.

Next, after listening to the lawyer, ask yourself, "Does this person seem to care?" The best doctors, lawyers, builders, and even car mechanics are people who take great pride in what they do and care about their clients/patients/customers. True professionals are not just people who have the skills and apply them. A true professional wants to leave you satisfied with their results, not just because it's good business, but because leaving you satisfied makes them happy too.

All things being equal, go with the lawyer that seems the most "passionate." Let's look at why. An old saying among lawyers is that "in divorce court, everyone lies." Even people who are as honest as they come will "stretch the truth" when it comes to divorce court and rationalize it to themselves as "justified." Clients are angry and hurt. They know that a decision that could affect the rest of their lives is in someone else's hands and many/most will say whatever they think they must in order to get the result they want. The judges and hearing officers know this and have to rely heavily on their own instincts to determine what the truth is. A passionate lawyer has a huge edge when it comes to swinging that pendulum in your favor. I have actually had judges tell me after a trial that they were on the line but went my way, because they thought that, if I was that passionate about my position, I must be right.

One warning to keep in mind about passionate lawyers though, 90% of divorce cases settle. A good settlement is your real goal. Cases that do not settle are far more expensive than they need to be. A lawyer's passion needs to be tempered with common sense. The worst thing a lawyer can do to their client is to get so invested in their client's story that they lose the ability to compromise a little and negotiate effectively. I may take a lot of heat for saying this, but this failing, in my own personal experience, happened more often with female divorce lawyers (not all of them) than with their male counterparts. Generally speaking, the female lawyers were better than the men at being empathetic and truly caring about their clients, but many were just not as good at knowing when to step back and effectively negotiate.

Conservative Judge Clancy.
I knew that Judge Clancy was a devout Roman Catholic. He had nine children and, in his chambers, was a picture of him with the Pope. There was no doubt in my mind that this judge was not liberal minded. It was no accident that, when I represented Bill, a doctor whose wife had left him for another woman, this case ended up in front of him.

Responsible Judge Reynolds.
Judge Reynolds was estranged from his wife and rumors were that he had found a new love and moved out of his marital home. Again, no coincidence that a case where my client was a wife whose husband was seeing someone else but refused to move out of the marital home ended up in front of him when I was seeking an exclusive possession order for her. I still remember his expression as he looked down at the husband and said, "Look, not all marriages last forever but you need to man up and stop rubbing her nose in it."

Compassionate Judge Carlyle.
Judge Carlyle had four adult daughters. My client's husband had moved out and emptied the marital home while she was in the hospital giving birth. I could see the judge's eyes glaring at the husband as I told the story. I then told her that I had previously

gotten an order freezing the marital bank accounts but that my client needed some money to re-furnish the house. She asked how much I needed, and I answered $75,000. The used furniture the husband had removed was probably worth 20% of that amount. She then ordered that $150,000.00 be taken from the marital account with half credited against each party. Then she ordered the husband's half be turned over to the wife so she could replace furniture. The husband's lawyer later commented to me privately how lucky I was to have that issue end up in front of Judge Carlyle. I smiled to myself, thinking, luck is something that you have to make yourself.

A final consideration with any prospective lawyer is whether they have the common sense to get to know the judges and how they have used that information to benefit their clients. Ask the lawyer to name all the judges that could potentially get your case and ask the lawyer to tell you about each one. Finally, ask the lawyer how he or she has used this knowledge in the past to help his or her clients.

A good lawyer knows the law; a great lawyer knows the judge.

2

Physical, Mental, and Financial Abuse

Safety matters.

Throughout this book I have included humorous recollections of actual events, but in this section, I have only serious stories to share. I will always remember as if it were yesterday my 23 year old client, who, when she answered the door holding her two-year-old daughter in her arms, was shot and killed by her husband who had just received his divorce papers. Her two-year-old was not physically hurt. The husband then put the gun to his own head and killed himself. Throughout my career, there seemed to be at least one death per year among my clients that was not from natural causes.

I also recall my client who visited me right before my firm's Christmas break and shared that her husband had beaten her, leaving a huge black and blue bruise on her cheek. She added that her husband then took a knife and destroyed all of her clothing and continued his assault, going to the garage, opening the hood of her car, and cutting up all the wiring. I rushed to court with her and got a protection order (also known as a restraining order in some states) that evicted him from the marital home and gave her temporary custody of her children and temporary financial support. A deputy sheriff went to his workplace, served him with a court order, and explained in detail that, if he were to return to the home, he would be arrested for violating the order and jailed for six months. Three days later, my client called him and begged him to come back and then called me asking me to discontinue the court order that kept him away from her.

Physical Abuse

Thankfully, physical abuse only seemed to be an issue in about one in thirty cases, but I always made it a point to discuss this subject with every client at the beginning of every initial consultation. Many clients were too embarrassed to bring it up themselves, while others would not talk about it unless asked because they had been "brainwashed" or conditioned by their spouses to accept abuse as "normal."

My initial question was, "Has there ever been a time when your spouse hit you or your children, or slapped you or your children, or shoved you or your children, or pushed you/your children, or forced you to have sex when you did not want to, or touched you in any way without your consent? Has there ever been a time when your spouse threatened you or your children with any form of physical harm or death?" In almost every single state, an answer of yes to any of these questions would meet the definition of physical abuse.

Occasionally my client had the foresight to take pictures of herself showing bruises or other injuries she had sustained, but this was the rare exception. In most cases, the abuser would never reveal himself by doing these things in front of others, and he would make sure that there was no visible evidence of the abuse. The vast majority of abuse cases were just one person's word (testimony) against the other person's denials. Thankfully, most judges will give the victim of the abuse the benefit of the doubt and assume they are telling the truth. Judges know that there is rarely any evidence other than the statements of the victims, and they also know that it is better to err in favor of the victim and grant an order of protection.

In most states, unless there are serious injuries that require medical intervention, the protection order procedures are civil rather than criminal remedies. This means that a protection order will generally not cause the abuser to have a criminal record or lose his job. Instead, the order the court issues will simply serve to separate the parties and hopefully calm the situation. This is why most judges will just take the abuse victim's word for what happened and issue a court order. In many states, besides immediately evicting the abuser, the orders will also authorize the police officer to take all guns from the accused abuser. Victims of abuse should always remember though that a court order is still only a piece of paper that, although often effective, is also often ignored. Many abusers assume that their spouse will not have the internal strength to call the police and report a violation. Like a little kid testing authority, many abusers will violate the court order by calling the victim or showing up at the home or at their work "just to talk." It is critical for the abuse victim to call the police and report every single one of these violations or the abuser will likely assume that the order means nothing and the violations will escalate.

In most states there is a procedure in place so that an abuse victim can get a court order without even needing an attorney. Every lawyer who practices family law will know exactly what steps should be taken by the victim. Most of these protection or restraining orders will evict the abuser and, if requested by the victim, can also award temporary custody of the children and temporary financial support. In most cases, the initial or first order will be given without the abuser even knowing about the hearing. These first orders will be temporary and only be effective until the date of a second hearing where the abusing spouse will have the opportunity to come to court and defend themselves. At the second hearing, the judge will usually enter a final order that will be effective for a much longer period of time. If the abusing spouse does not show up, so long as he has been served with the notice of the hearing, a final order will be entered in his absence. Even if he does show up, in most cases, the judges will listen to the abusing spouse's defense and denials and then go with the victim's word and enter an order.

Important note.

Your spouse will often claim that the abuse never happened and that you are just a "conniving" and overly emotional woman who is trying to "game" the court. If you did not call the police, you did not go to an emergency room, or you did not take action as quickly as possible, the opposing counsel may claim that you were not really in fear for your safety and that the incident didn't really happen. Sadly, unless there are visible bruises or injuries, the police may not be as effective as they should be. I would suggest that you do call the police and that you do get medical help, but I would also suggest you also follow up quickly by seeking a restraining/protective order, regardless of what the police say and even if there are no serious injuries that can be easily seen by the medical providers. The judge will have to decide if you are really scared and if you have good reason to be. Your job here is to act in a way that shows them that you are scared. This means calling the police and getting medical help. Take pictures and get copies of medical records and police reports as soon as you can. You should also know that when children are the possible victims of abuse by an adult/parent, the police will usually get a local governmental agency involved to do their own investigation. This will usually be a social worker who will interview you, the children, and the other spouse. Cooperate fully with the social worker and make sure that you and the children give them as much information as possible.

If you or your children are the victim of abuse by your spouse, my recommendations when it comes to documenting what happened, filling out the forms, and testifying in court are as follows:

Start by writing down the date and approximate time of the most recent incident of abuse. Then, describe what happened. You do not need to go into intricate detail about an argument and relate who said what; instead, you can just say, "we had an argument," and then follow up with a lot of details relating to the actual abuse that occurred and describe the resulting pain or injury. Remember, in most states, physical abuse is defined as being hit, slapped, pushed, shoved, or forced to have sex without your consent. Often, being threatened with any physical harm or death is also considered abuse.

If you called the police or told anyone about the incident right after it happened, include this information on the forms you fill out and report this when you testify at any hearings. Of course, if any marks were left on you and you took pictures, bring them.

Don't be afraid to show emotion. Crying and describing your fear will help. If you use a monotone or "clinical" voice this may be interpreted by the judge as not being a serious issue, since you don't seem too shaken up.

If there were other incidents in the past, describe them. Start with the one most recent to the last abuse and work backwards in time. Give an approximate date or time period (you can even say "last summer" if you don't recall the exact date), then follow up with the detailed description of the touching or threat as well as detail regarding the resulting pain and/or injury. Remember, treat each touching without consent or threat of harm as a separate incident and talk about each one, giving the date or approximate time period, and then go on to describe what happened. Don't be afraid to add extra pages to any form; better to have included more incidents than to have left things out.

Describe your fear of possible future abuse. If your spouse has issues with controlling his anger, talk about this, and if there are other incidents that are not necessarily directed at you or your children, such as road rage, etc., describe them.

In many states, the court has the power to order your spouse out of the marital residence because of the abuse. This is called eviction or giving you exclusive possession of the residence. Often, it does not matter who owns the residence or whether it is rented, leased, or owned. Additionally, in many states, the court can also give you temporary custody, and the court can order your spouse to start paying you financial support. If you want the court to order your spouse out of the house and you need custody or financial support, be sure to ask for them on the forms you fill out and when you appear before the judge, right after you have described the abuse.

Obtaining a Protection or Restraining Order

In many states, the procedural steps to get a protection or restraining order are as follows:

1. Fill out forms describing what happened using the methods described above. If a lawyer or another person fills out the paperwork, be sure to read it very carefully and make sure that every detail is accurate and that nothing has been left out. Even if the lawyer or court employee tells you there is enough there, insist that all of your narrative be included. If you want your spouse removed from the residence, if you want custody of the children, and if you want financial support, be sure to write this down after you have written about the abuse on the paperwork or forms.

2. Appear before a judge or hearing officer without your spouse present to get a temporary order. Here you should verbally describe what happened telling about the most recent incident as well as the past ones. Don't be afraid to show your emotions. If you have pictures showing injuries or copies of medical or police reports, bring them. If you cannot get copies of these reports for the first hearing, try to have them in your hands for the 2nd hearing.

3. Appear before a judge or hearing officer for a second hearing during which your spouse will be given a chance to come and tell his/her side of the story. It is important that you repeat everything you wrote down in the forms and describe everything the same way you did at the first hearing. Again, show emotion when you testify, even though you may not feel it as strongly now, after having repeated the story so many times. Be sure to bring pictures and copies of police and medical reports if you have them.

As stated previously, it is critically important that, once you get a court order, you take it upon yourself to see that it's enforced regardless of how minuscule you think the infraction might be. If the order prohibits the abusing spouse from calling you (and most protective orders do this), you need to immediately call the police and report every violation. The first words out of your mouth when you call the police should be, "I have a protection order or I have a restraining order signed by judge _____ dated _____." Then proceed to tell the 911 operator what your spouse has done that violates the terms of that order.

If you fail to enforce the court order, several negative things can happen. First and foremost, the abusing spouse may feel emboldened and justified in continuing to violate the order in a more serious manner, and, even if you do later call the police to report the more serious violations, your spouse may claim that you were also at fault since you ignored the order too. In addition, if you fail to seek enforcement of the order when a smaller violation occurs, the judge may later determine that you are not in that much fear for your safety and end the order. If the court order protects your children because there has been abuse against them, the judge may hold it against you for not doing your duty in protecting them.

Understanding Abuse and the Abuser

The second story I told at the beginning of this chapter tells about an abused wife who had the court protection order dismissed and went back to her husband. Unfortunately, this is a common occurrence. This pattern, in which a spouse commits abuse, then expresses remorse and asks for forgiveness, and then convinces the victim that what happened is partly or wholly her fault, is one that I have seen too many times. If you think you or your children might be a victim of abuse, I would strongly recommend that you go online and search the term "understanding spousal abuse" and "the Duluth Model of Power and Control." You can also call the National Domestic Violence Hotline at 1-800-799-7233. Additional resources are listed in Appendix D and E.

You will find that there are similar patterns that occur in abusive relationships and that the abuser's desire for control is a common theme. The patterns are a predictable escalation that is often so subtle a victim may not even realize that it is happening to them. There is, however, a clear "cycle," and educating yourself about what is going on and what resources are available to you can actually save your life.

Mental and Financial Abuse

Although the courts in most states are set up to deal with

physical abuse and threats of physical harm, they are often not good at dealing with mental and emotional abuse. It is important that you fully describe what you are experiencing to the attorney in the initial consultation even if you feel embarrassed or ashamed.

The most common scenario I saw in clients who I felt were victims of emotional abuse was one in which a spouse regularly said things to belittle and diminish the other spouse's self-esteem. The emotionally abusing spouse's goal was to assume more and more control over the victim. The abusing spouse achieved this by convincing the victim that she had no choice but to accept this form of abuse because she was to blame, she was worthless, and she could not survive without him. My recommended first step if you are experiencing abuse is to seek counseling. The second step is to develop and work on an *exit plan*. Money can be the lifeblood of freedom, and an important part of the exit plan is to begin finding ways to hide away some funds, even if it means putting away a few dollars each week.

A third step is to educate yourself about your rights and where you would stand legally if you were to separate and eventually divorce. Even if you think a separation or divorce is not in your immediate future, quietly visit some lawyers who specialize in family law, and do your best to get an education from them. Knowledge is power and knowing the likely procedures and results if you do leave can often give you immense strength.

While women who are victims of physical abuse may show bruises and other clear evidence of their abuse, women who are victims of emotional abuse often feel helpless, because there is no clear evidence of the emotional abuse that they can show anyone else. Because of this, the courts are often not prepared to offer any substantial relief for emotional abuse. In these situations, a clear, detailed journal in which the wife writes down the date and a description of what happened and what her husband did or said can be very useful to her attorney. One single incident or single example of emotional abuse on its own may seem trivial to an outsider, but a diary/journal documenting multiple incidents can be a useful tool for a skilled attorney.

Many times, the emotional abuse has gone on for so long that the woman who is the victim of it considers the emotional abuse "normal." These women are the ones most in need of a skilled counselor, and these women are also the ones who are most likely to accept a settlement that is far less than they are entitled to, just to conclude the divorce process as quickly as possible.

It is important to remember that a final divorce decree is just a piece of paper that allows you to marry someone else. If you are not in a big hurry to marry someone else, it is more important to let your lawyer have the time he or she needs to properly get you all that you are entitled to.

3

Should I Stay or Should I Go?

The best advice.
My wife and I had been separated for about nine months when she showed up at my door in tears, begging me to reconcile and give our marriage another try. I responded that I would give it some thought and then I sought advice from four people: my mother, my brother, my sister, and my best friend Frank.

My mother immediately replied: "Of course you have to take her back and try again, she is the mother of your children." My brother Dan stated, "Are you crazy? You have never been happy in that marriage. Why would you take her back?" My sister Lynne offered, "I would suggest that you not make a quick decision. Take a least a month and think about it." Finally, my best friend Frank, who was born and raised in Alabama and who has been married several times himself, said in his endearing, southern drawl; "Jon, if you have a chance not to split your money in half, you have got to reconcile."

I did agree to reconcile, and we agreed to do our best to make the marriage work. We lasted another six months together and then separated for the last time. One of the things that I observed over and over again in my divorce practice is that, if a client had not physically separated from her spouse when she came to me for advice and divorce education, she was far more successful when it came to healing and repairing her marriage. I saw many times that, once a couple was truly, physically separated and were no longer under the same roof, the probability of a successful reconciliation went way down. I think that many felt that being separated and living outside the marriage was not as scary as they thought it would be, so when unresolved issues and problems arose again, the fear of leaving did not hold them back.

The remainder of Chapter 3 was contributed by licensed clinical psychologist, Dr. Elizabeth Jenkins.

So, You Are Considering a Divorce

To stay or not stay; it is rarely an easy decision. Most people believe that they will be among the 50% whose marriages will succeed. When people get married, none of them do so believing that they will be unhappy enough, dissatisfied enough, or angry enough that divorce will emerge as a very real possibility. None of us marry with a plan to divorce within the first 10 years or so, and yet more than 50% of us do just that.

You probably married your partner reassured by a belief that you had found your "happily ever after." You believed that you had teamed up with someone for life, one whom you would always like, would always find as funny and attractive and loving as the day you fell in love, and one with whom that feeling of connectedness and trust and optimism for the future would continue. You believed that your marriage would be the one that succeeded... yet now, you're not so sure.

You are ultimately the only person who can make this decision about what is best for you. As nice as it would be if your best friend or your mom or your counselor or this book could tell you how to proceed and what the "right" decision is, they can't. Right now, though, you may not feel equipped to even answer the question yourself.

Part of the reason this choice is so challenging is that, generally, there is no one right choice for whether to stay or leave a marriage. A multitude of factors warrant consideration. The best advice as you wrestle with this decision is to give yourself the time you need to collect information so the decision that you do make will be an informed one. This will likely involve examining your feelings, your behaviors, your support system, your financial resources, your safety, your values, and your children's needs if you have children.

Aysha.

My close friend Aysha confided in me several years ago that she was considering leaving her husband after 25 years of marriage. They were college sweethearts. There was no physical or emotional abuse. They weren't angry with one another, nor were they in a disagreement about finances, child rearing, or values. There was no substance abuse. No one had been unfaithful. However, through their years together, the passion had all but disappeared. Physical displays of affection were absent. Sex was non-existent. Aysha wondered about the possibilities that might exist beyond marriage. She wanted to feel desirable; she wanted to experience passion once again. After toying with the idea of divorce, talking to her husband about the options, and considering all the pros and cons that she could identify, she and her husband decided to remain married. Why? After much consideration, the couple recognized that the two of them prioritized one very important value: raising their children in a loving and fully supportive environment. This was the driving force in their decision to stay together, despite their dispassionate relationship. They determined that they were a good team when it came to parenting, with a mutual love for their children, a strong respect for one another, and a commitment to their roles as parents. Years later, they appear very much at peace with their decision, and for them it was the "right" decision.

Cyndi.
Another friend, Cyndi, grieved over her decision to divorce her husband Al. She loved him very much and had for many years. They had one child whom they were both crazy about. Their relationship was filled with passion. However, Cyndi's husband struggled with significant alcohol and prescription medication abuse. His substance use was significant enough that Cyndi had concerns for her son's safety when he spent time with his father. What if his father were to drive while intoxicated and have an accident with him in the car? Cyndi made a very difficult decision to separate from Al. For several years, Al attempted to recover from his addiction, with only brief periods of success. Eventually, Cyndi divorced Al and maintained full custody of her son. Her husband was granted supervised visitation when sober.

Six months after the divorce, Al appeared to have achieved a prolonged period of sobriety. Months went by and he did not drink alcohol or take controlled drugs. One evening, Al returned home after having completed a several-hour, supervised visit with his son and took several narcotics and anti-anxiety medications prescribed by a new physician he had begun seeing. Then he broke out the alcohol and drank late into the night. The next day, family members found him dead in his own bed, having choked on his own vomit.

Sarah.
A third friend, Sarah, married her partner of several years, a highly respected professional in the community. Shortly after the birth of their first child, her husband James became irritable, critical, and began working late and unpredictable hours. A few years went by, and the couple engaged in couples therapy and had a second child. James gradually became more angry and critical. He assumed control of the money that Sarah earned and limited her access, stating that she was too irresponsible with money. His work hours became longer and more unpredictable. He frequently

left town on business. He criticized Sarah's relationships with her friends and family members. He asked her to quit her job. Sarah began to have difficulty paying for basic necessities like food and medications. Attempts to discuss the financial situation usually ended with James becoming enraged, yelling obscenities, threatening to restrict more of her access to money, and storming out of the house. Sarah began to experience a growing fear for her safety and the safety of her children. She was embarrassed that she had not seen the early signs of an abusive marriage and that she had allowed things to progress to this point. Eventually, Sarah found out that her husband was in a relationship with another woman and that he had been spending most of the money Sarah earned to maintain the second relationship. Sarah and James separated, and eventually Sarah filed for divorce. After a lengthy and painful several years in and out of court, the divorce was finalized, and Sarah and James maintained shared custody.

As you consider the possibility that you will be getting a divorce, a good question to ask yourself as you wonder about how you should proceed is:

What is it that I need? What am I hoping for by getting divorced?

If your initial response is that you want to be happy, that you just want a change, or that you want more romance or passion in your life, then divorce may not be your best choice. Divorce is certainly not a guarantee for happiness; it is not a bargaining chip or something to casually threaten; there is nothing romantic about it. While it will induce change, exactly what that change will look like is anyone's guess. Divorce will not lead to "happily ever after," especially if children are involved. It is a life altering process. It is not a single event. It continues, long after the decree is signed by the judge. Neither marriage nor divorce will make you happy, and divorce, like marriage, usually involves periods of intense unhappiness. It will likely change everything in your life. It is never easy, and it generally involves great loss. That said, sometimes divorce is the only viable option, despite the messes that it tends to create. Divorce may provide you with an opportunity to heal, help you to find safety, or allow for the possibility of loving again.

I once shared with a friend who was considering divorce as a solution to a less than passionate period in her marriage my belief that one should never enter divorce unless he or she would prefer to live under a bridge than to stay in the marital relationship. Brutal? Yes. True? Possibly. If you were tired of your outdated home décor and longed for an update, you probably wouldn't opt for bull-dozing your home as a first option. Neither should one choose divorce as the first solution to marital difficulties. The idea that "grass is always greener on the other side" really does warrant consideration when it comes to divorce. Getting divorced does not mean that you will be happier, feel less alone, or be more financially secure. Sure, these outcomes are possible, but potentially at a very high cost.

That said, let's review some basic facts:

1. You have a right to feel safe.
2. You have a right to feel (or not) your feelings about the situation.
3. No feelings are permanent, and intimacy will naturally ebb and flow.
4. There is no such thing as "happily ever after." There is, however, good enough.
5. You are ultimately responsible for how you choose to behave towards yourself, your spouse, and any children that you have, and your spouse is responsible for how he chooses to behave.
6. Choosing divorce does not mean that you are a failure.

What Makes Relationships Fail?

Most of us were raised on fairy tales. The Cinderella story inaugurated many of us into the idea that marriage is the beginning of our "happily ever after." Few of us are prepared for the challenges that we will encounter during our marriages, and there is no manual to guide us. We generally "fly by the seat of our pants" and pray for the best. For some, this is enough. For others, the train derails, and solutions seem to lie just beyond a couple's reach. Often, there seems to be no rhyme or reason for why some marriages succeed or fail, and at other times the reasons seem quite clear.

A wonderful book about what predicts the success or failure of relationships and how to shift the odds towards a successful one is John Gottman's *Why Marriages Succeed or Fail: And How You Can Make Yours Last* (1995). In his book, Gottman reassures us that it is not simply the presence of conflict that predicts which marriages are doomed for failure. Conflict in relationships is, in fact, very normal. Instead, it is about how this conflict typically is or isn't resolved that can be telling. In his book, Gottman refers to "the four horsemen of the apocalypse": *criticism, defensiveness, contempt,* and *stonewalling.* While these responses to conflict will occur occasionally in most relationships, they occur less frequently in healthy relationships, and partners in healthy relationships tend to work harder to repair these rifts when they do occur. In this and several other Gottman books on relationships, he introduces ways to improve relationships by avoiding these styles of interacting.

Why Do People Seek a Divorce?

Believe it or not, cheating is not the number one reason for divorce. While surveys suggest that at least 70% of men and women have cheated on their spouses, infidelity generally represents a symptom of a bigger problem, not the problem itself. Frequently, couples describe lack of communication as the primary cause of the marriage's demise. Often couples will cite growing apart and having developed different interests as the reason for the divorce. Marrying for the wrong reasons, disappointed expectations, discord, financial strain, and lack of passion are also named as sources for marital demise.

Sometimes a marriage is heavily taxed by external stressors that occur. The death of a child, the loss of a job, or a serious illness may push an otherwise healthy marriage to its breaking point, and counseling can be important in order for the relationship to endure. Even if the relationship doesn't survive the crisis, counseling may assist the couple in parting kindly and without additional discord.

When abuse is occurring in a relationship, safety becomes the primary concern, and ending the relationship may be the only way to ensure the well-being of everyone involved. In the event of abuse, it becomes important to consider a safety plan, as the risks to safety tend to increase when the abused party attempts to leave.

Where to Begin

While there are additional considerations in certain situations, such as risk to the safety of you or your children, generally the smartest course of action when considering divorce is to slow down, consider the answers to several questions, and begin collecting essential information about what the process of divorce will entail.

Why do you want a divorce?

Asking yourself why you want a divorce is a good place to start. Are you unhappy in your marriage or is it your choice of partner that you are unhappy with? Unhappy marriages are not necessarily irreconcilable marriages. In fact, with renewed communication, acceptance of differences, and commitment to the relationship, often with the assistance of a counselor, the marriage may improve significantly. You may want to reconsider "[throwing] out the baby with the bathwater" if an improved relationship is your primary goal.

Are you avoiding pain?

Healthy marriages require a willingness to face pain. Ironically, so do healthy divorces. Remember the saying, "wherever you go, there you are." Before deciding that divorce is the answer, do an honest inventory and consider sources other than your spouse that may be contributing to your pain.

Have you sought out quality help from a counselor?

"If at first you don't succeed, try, try again" (Hickson, et al., 1984). A good couple's therapist can be invaluable as you and your spouse attempt to determine your future as a couple. Whether the two of you decide to stay together or part ways, a good therapist can help you follow through with your choices in a manner that is respectful and consistent with your values. If children are involved, a good therapist can help both of you to remain mindful of one of your biggest priorities, the well-being of the children. Keep in mind that children are not damaged so much by the presence of conflict or disagreement between parents as they are by the manner in which those disagreements are resolved. Asking for help as you learn skills in resolving conflict respectfully will go a long way in softening the emotional punch that a divorce has on children. It is also a set of skills that you will take with you into the future, whether it is in your marriage or in another relationship.

Have you encountered stressors that are so great they have pushed your relationship to the edge?

All marriages are tested during times of stress. However, some stressors are so significant or severe that they are likely to threaten even the healthiest of relationships. During periods of extreme stress or loss such as the death of a family member, financial challenges, or serious illness, counseling with a therapist or spiritual leader may provide needed support, particularly when both spouses are in crisis and therefore less able to provide support to one another. Even if the marriage cannot survive, letting go does not require contempt; there is no rule that says that you must leave a post-hurricane path of destruction if the relationship ends.

Have you taken an honest inventory of your own behaviors in the relationship?

I've seen many relationships destroyed when a partner sets impossible standards for his or her partner ("he should..., he shouldn't ..."). This "shoulding" all over your spouse is a recipe for failure. Our expectation of what an ideal partner will be in a relationship is usually based on our own experiences growing up, whether we model our expectations after the relationship we saw our parents have or we react to what we saw in our parents' relationship by seeking the opposite. However, when you create a set of rules for how a partner "ought to" behave in a relationship (and they for you), you have just made that person responsible for your own emotional well-being, and the responsibility for whether or not you feel good or bad now rests in another person's hands, leaving you powerless to change your own experience.

Often when you find yourself feeling disappointed or angry about a partner's behavior, it can be helpful to ask yourself, "What can I do to help myself feel better?" or "How can I improve this situation for myself?" This exercise shifts your focus back onto something you do have control over... your own actions. This may mean being willing to speak honestly and directly about difficulties and assume responsibility for feeling better rather than quickly reacting with blame. Rarely is a conflict as simple as one person's "fault," and focusing on how you yourself can improve a bad situation is much more likely to leave you feeling better than angrily (and helplessly) waiting for your partner to change.

Assuming responsibility for your own emotional well-being is not the same as accepting fault or settling for hurtful behavior. Taking responsibility for your well-being simply means that you are ultimately responsible for your choices and behaviors and that there are steps you can take to feel better, and your partner is responsible for their choices and behaviors as well. Although focusing on what we ourselves can do to feel better is essential to the success of a marriage, the process of divorce tends to encourage the opposite focus: a defensive stance that concentrates on the failings in our partner's behavior. Once this focus on who's to blame begins, it can be a difficult position to move past.

Do you want revenge, or do you want to feel better?

In the movies, revenge may be sweet, but, in real life, it rarely eases pain. Add children to the mix, and revenge tends to not only bite the hand that seeks it but also hurt the children whose sense of self is a reflection of both parents. Hurt the parent; hurt the child. Criticize the parent and you are, in effect, criticizing the child. A good motto is "Do you want to be right or do you want to be healthy?"

What will the logistics of divorce actually look like? What will you lose?

This is an important question, as divorce is not a pleasant

experience. You are likely to lose money, your home, belongings, friends, and even time with your children in divorce, and it is important that you enter this new phase in life with your eyes wide open. Preparing for these losses in advance will go a long way towards helping you to rebuild on the other side.

Are you or your children being injured or hurt?

As presented in the previous chapter, a critical consideration when examining the future of your relationship is choosing the appropriate course of action when there is abuse. Whether or not an individual should leave an abusive relationship is not a simple one. Abuse can emerge in various ways including using intimidation; emotional abuse; using isolation; using minimizing, denying, and blaming; using children; economic abuse; or using coercion and threats. *Domestic violence* is a pattern of behaviors used by one partner to maintain power and control over another partner in an intimate relationship. It is a process rather than an event. Domestic violence does not always appear overnight. Too often, it begins more insidiously, with behaviors that are intended to gain power and control and that intensify over time. The risk for physical violence often increases right after the victim leaves, which is why it is so important to develop a safety plan first.

Common themes in domestic violence include:

1. A belief that the abused can change the abuser
2. Guilt, feelings of failure, and self-blame
3. Depression and low self-esteem and self-worth
4. Fear of financial repercussions
5. Fear of losing custody of the children
6. Fear of what the abuser will do if the abused leaves
7. Lack of information about resources for support

Figure 1. The Power and Control Wheel

From "The Duluth Model Power and Control Wheel," by the
Domestic Abuse Intervention Project, (Retrieved from
http://theduluthmodel.org). Reprinted with permission.

The Duluth Model of Power and Control (DAIP, 202 East
Superior St., Duluth, Minnesota, 55802; 1981) in Figure 1
shows how perpetrators use different ways to exert power and
control over those they choose to abuse. The bottom line: it is
all about power and control, and physical violence is not the
only type of abuse.

Returning to the question, "Am I or are my children being injured or hurt?" What should you do if you find yourself in a situation involving domestic violence? As you begin to define your goals, some important questions to ask are:

1. *Where are my current supports?*
2. *What don't I know that I need to know?*
3. *Where can I start my search for information (e.g., counselor, physician, attorney, shelter, library)?*
4. *What facts about myself do I need to begin to accept?*
5. *How can I begin to build up additional support, so that I can be better prepared to take care of myself (and children) moving forward?*
6. *What might my safety plan look like?*

For additional information, visit Appendices C and D.

In summary, divorce is probably one of the biggest decisions that you will ever make, and there are no easy answers. The decision about whether to seek a divorce is a very personal one. You are your own best expert, and you are the only one who can truly decide the best course of action. Your decision should be made carefully, with your eyes wide open, armed with information and support. Divorce does not mean that you are a failure. You are not automatically a bad person because you choose divorce. In fact, choosing different paths for you and your spouse may be the most loving option of all. Many times, the actual divorce itself is a formality. The marriage may have died long before the divorce even occurs, and it takes courage to acknowledge that fact. With mindful consideration of all involved parties and a commitment to behaving in a manner that is consistent with your values, divorce may be your best, next step.

4

Custody

The bluff.
Many years ago, I had a client named Cathy who told me that, whenever she and her children arrived home, the very first thing she did was run ahead of her children to erase the obscene messages her estranged husband would leave on the phone's answering machine so that the children would not hear them. Of course, my first question was, "Do you have any of these tapes?" and she sadly replied that she did not as she had always immediately erased them.

On the day of the trial, about half an hour before noon, it was my turn to cross examine the husband. I launched into questions about his hostility towards his wife and how the children were being impacted. I asked him if he had ever directed obscenities at his wife in front of the children, and he denied that he ever had. I then asked him if he had ever left hate-filled, obscene, voice messages on the answering machine. Again, he denied that he had. I followed up by asking him about whether he had left very specific phrases (ones that his wife had shared with me previously), such as, "You are such a lying c**nt" and "Are you going to teach our daughter to be a whore like you?" He continued to deny that he had ever used phrases like that. Next, I said, "Mr. Rivers, just to be clear, are you saying that you never left a voice message on your wife's home answering machine, where you know your children might hear them? Are you denying that you said in so many words that your wife was a lying c**nt and a whore?" He again denied leaving such messages. Following these denials, the judge announced that we were going to break for lunch.

During lunch, I walked back to my office and placed a portable cassette player into my briefcase. Then I walked out to my car parked behind the building and took out four cassette tapes: two Bruce Springsteen and two Bob Dylan.

At 1:30, we were back in court and the judge invited me to resume my cross examination. I began with "Mr. Rivers, do you understand that you are under oath here?" He said yes. I then said, "You do understand, don't you, that the penalty for lying under oath in a court of law includes imprisonment?" At this point his lawyer objected, and I quickly said, "I am withdrawing the question," and I walked back to the counsel table where my client was sitting. I opened my briefcase that I had placed on the table rather than placing it on the floor next to the table like I normally did. I made sure that I stood slightly to the side so that the husband could clearly see what I was doing, and I removed the portable tape player from my briefcase and set it on the table.

Next, I took out the four cassette tapes and placed them next to the tape player. I then turned back and faced the husband on the stand, paused a moment, and then stated very slowly and clearly, "Mr. Rivers, I am going to ask you one last time, did you ever leave obscene messages on your wife's home phone answering machine?" I could see the blood had drained out of his face as he hung his head down and answered almost just above a whisper, "Yes, yes I did." Of course, I responded to his whisper, "I'm sorry, I had trouble hearing that answer. Could you answer a little louder please?" to which he almost shouted, "Yes, I did!" At this point I continued asking questions to obtain confirmation from *him that had in fact used all of the obscene phrases his wife had shared with me, and I also asked him to acknowledge that his kids could have possibly heard his messages.*

Years later at a Bar luncheon, I was seated next to the judge who had presided over that trial, and I shared with him about how Bruce Springsteen and Bob Dylan had made it into his courtroom. He practically doubled over laughing and then asked me, "What if the husband had kept up his denials and called your bluff?" I answered that I would have simply moved on to another subject, figuring my client would have been no worse off. Of course, I had never represented to the court that I had the answering machine tapes. The implication was all I needed.

Determining What is in the Best Interest of the Children

No minor children? Skip this chapter and say a prayer of gratitude. The bottom line is that all children lose in a divorce, some just a lot more than others.

Keep in mind that I am not suggesting couples with minor children should always stay together. If one or both parents are chronically unhappy in the relationship, the children will know this and getting them out of that environment will often do them less harm than staying in it.

Your role as a parent is to properly guide your children to adulthood; you have no greater responsibility. Your primary job is to do everything in your power to help your children achieve their full potential in every way possible.

The law regarding custody and visitation in every state is somewhat uniform. The key principle that will guide every judge and that should also guide every parent is, "What's in the best interest of the children?" If a judge finds that the scales are not tipped in favor of one parent over another, he will often consider a second factor, "Which parent is more likely to foster and encourage the children's relationship with the other parent?"

In my family law practice, there came a time when I would not do any more custody battles. I turned over all the custody work to the younger lawyers in my firm, because I just got tired of seeing children lose. Make no mistake about it, children will always lose when their own parents cannot recognize and do what is best for them and must resort to using a stranger (the judge, court appointed social worker, or psychologist) to make decisions for them.

The custody/visitation courts are only needed when one or both parents cannot put their children's needs ahead of their own. Of course, many parents will rationalize that they are really doing what is best for their children, when, sadly, they are so wrapped up in their own anger that they are not really putting their children first.

The bottom line is that, in a divorce, when it comes to their children, parents should be the ones who come together and decide what type of schedule will best fit their children's needs. Since this is not always possible for a variety of reasons, the family courts must step in and make this decision for the parents.

Types of Custody

Let's review the terms and options available to the courts:

Legal Custody. Having the legal right to make and participate in all major decisions concerning the children.

Physical Custody. Having the children in your possession.

Partial Custody. A portion of the total custody time with the children is assigned to a parent. A common scenario assigns Primary Physical Custody to one parent and this is where the children will live the majority of the time, with the other parent having Partial Custody. Another common scenario is Shared Custody, with equal time spent between both parents and shared decision-making by both parents.

Time Sharing. Some states now refer to custody as time-sharing in an attempt to emphasize the importance of having both parents actively involved in the children's lives.

Visitation Schedule. Denotes a schedule in which a parent who does not have primary Physical Custody will have the children with them. This is often called a Partial Custody schedule.

Shared Legal Custody. This is the most common scenario in which both parents have the right to jointly make and participate in major decisions concerning the children.

Primary Legal Custody. One parent alone has the right to make all major decisions regarding the children. This is not common.

Primary Physical Custody. The children spend more than half the time with one parent. This parent is said to have Primary Physical Custody. This is quite common.

Shared Physical Custody. Often referred to as just Shared Custody, in this scenario the children spend equal amounts of time with each parent. Although not as common as one parent having Primary Physical Custody and the other having Partial Custody or visitation, this result is growing in popularity. Many psychologists believe this is the best result for the children, but it is only possible when both parents can fully put their children's needs first and cooperate with each other in a positive manner.

Remember that each state is different, and although the terms above are the most common, there may be variations in some states.

Settle, settle, settle... the sooner the better.

Thankfully, most of the time custody issues are settled by the children's parents. As I said earlier, this is the way it should be. Parents generally know what is in their children's best interests and bringing in strangers to make that decision for them should only be a last resort.

Using the courts to resolve your custody issues is expensive and an absolutely ridiculous way to flush money down the toilet. Even if you are so angry that you can't see straight, this is the one time when it is critical not to let your anger control your decision-making. The minute you know that you will not be living with your spouse, you will want to do your utmost to reach an agreement regarding your children. If you think you have an agreement or understanding, *write it down*, date it, and both of you sign it. Then, take the home-made agreement that is signed by both parents to an attorney and have that attorney make it legal for your state. Even if your spouse refuses to sign the agreement drawn up by the lawyer, the home-made agreement will still carry a lot of weight with the courts as long as you both signed and dated it.

Agreements regarding property division, child support, alimony, legal fees, etc., all take a back seat to reaching an agreement regarding custody. There is no rule that all issues need to be settled at the same time. So again, come to a meeting of the minds as to what is best for your children, write it down (known as *memorializing* it), and make sure that it is signed by both parents.

All that being said, don't focus on one tree to such an extent that you lose sight of the forest. This means that, although it is best if two parents can come to an agreement as to what is best for their children, one parent should not place so much value on the goal of settling that the resulting settlement is not really what will be best for the children. No one knows your children better than you do, so do not under any circumstances let yourself be pushed into any settlement that you do not truly feel will be best for them.

Mediation

Most court systems are now pushing or requiring some form of *mediation*. A family court mediator is usually an attorney or a therapist who has undergone specialized training in conflict resolution. The mediator will ideally save couples the time and the expense of going through a trial before a judge by getting the couple to recognize and agree to the likely result without going to court. It is important to remember, however, that mediators are expected to prevent most cases from going to court and thus some mediators may express a bias towards couples settling out of court, even when it is not in the best interest of both parties. For example, one parent may be more domineering, less accommodating, and rigid while the other parent may be more passive, and a mediocre mediator may respond to this by pushing the passive parent to concede to the demands of the more aggressive parent simply to achieve the settlement goal. The important thing that a parent involved in mediation must remember is to not compromise, unless they believe the result is the one that is best for their child.

Unfortunately, a scenario that is becoming increasingly common is that you will see a father who has not been equally involved in the children's lives pushing hard for a full shared custody agreement in which the children would spend an equal amount of time with each parent. While many psychologists opine that this can be the best result for the children, the truth is that full shared custody can be more harmful for the children than one parent having primary custody, if both parents cannot fully support one another in parenting and work collaboratively to ensure the well-being of the children. Too often, a father's true motivation in pushing for shared custody is that he has been told by his lawyer that this arrangement will greatly reduce or possibly even eliminate his child support obligation. Shared custody will have many challenges and if the children are accustomed to having one parent as their primary caretaker, the disruption can be harmful, especially when both parents are unable to work together to put their children's needs first. The bottom line is, do not settle for anything unless you genuinely believe that it will work in your situation.

Preserving the Status Quo

If it ain't broke, don't fix it

What you do with your children right after the separation makes a huge difference. Judges will assume that whatever arrangements regarding the children that have been in place were at least implicitly agreed upon by the parents and the children have adjusted to it. A parent who seeks to change the status quo will have an uphill battle, or, in legalese, the parent who wants a change will have a greater burden. This means that, if you wish to have primary physical custody of the children, it is important to set that up from the outset. The parent who wants to change things will have to show the court that there is a problem with just leaving things the way they are. Parents do have the right to seek a change in the custodial arrangement at any time, but once you have been doing things in a certain way, whether by agreement or court order, the parent who wants to change it will have the burden of showing

46

the court that a change will be in the best interests of the children and why.

Custody orders and custody agreements can always be revisited based on a change in circumstances, and the children being older and having different needs and desires can constitute a change in circumstances. Shared custody orders can also be changed if the court is convinced that the parents are just not capable of cooperating to the extent necessary. Of course, the parent seeking the change will have to show that they were not the one primarily at fault for the non-cooperation.

The Children's Wishes and Desires

A common question is: "Do the children's preferences about living arrangements carry any weight in determining the custody arrangement?" The short answer is "yes", the courts will take the children's wishes and desires into consideration, but those wishes are not the only factor influencing the decision. The judge will give more weight to a child's desires the older and more mature that child is. The judge will also explore the reasons for the child's preference to ensure that the choice is not the result of a parent's alienation efforts against the other parent. The judges will also look for evidence of coaching and direct attempts by a parent to buy the children's desires. Bottom line is that the judge must be the one making the decision, and the judge will be guided by his or her perception of what will be in the best interest of the children.

A big question is how the children's wishes will be communicated to the judge. The possible options are:

1. The children will testify directly before the judge. Although this is possible, it is not likely. Most judges do not like this option, since they feel it is putting the children in the terrible position of having to choose between their parents.

2. The more likely option is that the children will communicate their desires to some form of professional and that person will testify before the judge. The most common choices as to who this professional will be are as follows:

   a. A court-appointed, independent psychologist. This is often the best choice, but it is also the most expensive, and most of the time this option is not used because the parents cannot afford it. In my experience this option will cost somewhere between $3,000.00 and $20,000.00. Some judges will divide this cost based on the parents' incomes while others will just split it. Some will impose the entire cost on the parent who requests the psychologist's evaluation. Your lawyer should be able to discuss how often this option is used and how the cost is usually divided by the court. Your lawyer should also be able to tell you the names of the psychologists that the court most often uses and tell you his or her experiences with these individuals. Using a court appointed psychologist is my first choice if the parents can afford it.

   b. In another, more commonly used option, the court will appoint an independent non-psychologist to interview the children. This person can be a social worker or an individual who has undergone special training for this task. The position may be called a *guardian ad litem* or a *home study*. Here again, your lawyer should be able to tell you their experiences with this type of person and the costs involved.

Later in this chapter, I will discuss what you should communicate to the court appointed independent evaluator.

Getting Ready for a Fight

Your house will probably never burn down, yet it is always a good idea to have a fire extinguisher, smoke alarms, and fire insurance. Similarly, even if you think that custody will not be an issue and even if you have reached a written agreement on custody, a little insurance in the form of preparation if things don't work out is always a good idea.

Your lawyer may be the best there is, the fastest gun in the west, but no matter how good a shot or fast a gunslinger he or she is you must supply the ammunition. Without ammunition, the lawyer can never win the gunfight. Even if your lawyer is not that good, with enough ammunition, he has a decent chance of hitting the target and getting the results you want.

Organize and provide background information.

The first thing that you will need to provide your lawyer is the background information relating to the children, going back to the time you and your spouse were together. If you were the primary caretaker in that you were the one that was in charge of dealing with the children's doctors, teachers, and activities, it is important to detail this information and provide it to your lawyer. Similarly, if after the separation you have been the one primarily managing the children's doctors, teachers, and activities, detail this with as many specifics as possible.

At the outset, you should also be providing your lawyer with a detailed list as to why you believe the children should reside primarily with you, if that is your goal. If you express any opinions, it is important to list specific facts and detailed incidents and/or actions to support these opinions. For example, it's never enough to just write down that the other parent is a "wack-job" or that he is mentally "missing a few marbles" or that "his elevator just doesn't go to the top floor." These are all opinions. If you believe that your spouse is mentally unstable, be ready to provide your lawyer with a detailed account of your spouse's behaviors that led you to hold that belief.

Your background information should also include all issues and problems the other parent may have that you believe could have an impact on the best interests of the children. If the other parent struggles with alcohol or drug abuse, mental health issues, anger management issues, a history of poor judgment, or other forms of instability, all of these should be listed and detailed for your attorney.

When you prepare your outline of the background information, the first section of that outline should cover what the kids are used to, what has been their routine, and what role you have had in that routine. From there, the next section should address the problems listed in order of importance. If the other spouse has problems with mental/psychological issues, a history of substance, drug or alcohol abuse, criminal issues, or a history of domestic abuse, this is the next area that should be detailed. Then, the outline should detail other problems and issues, with details of disparagement and non-cooperation heading this list.

A final detail to include in your background outline, which is equally as important as detailing the other parent's problems, is a list of every possible issue or problem that you think the other parent might bring up about you. The worst thing that can happen to your lawyer is that he be surprised by information presented about you and thus unprepared to defend you. You must be totally honest and open with your lawyer in every way if you want him or her to be effective. Often, your lawyer will want to be the first to bring up some of your issues that might be perceived negatively by the court, so that he has the opportunity to soften and explain these issues.

The custody journal.

Your best ammunition/insurance is a detailed custody journal.

Set aside 10 minutes, every, single day, to write in that journal. Making journal entries within 24 hours of any problems is critical.

So, what should go into the custody journal? First, remember the factors that a court will use in a custody dispute: the best interest of the children and which parent is more likely to encourage a relationship with the other parent. Every time you feel that your spouse has not put the children's needs first or has done anything that you think is not in the best interests of your children, you need to write it down. Write down every example, if it occurs, of how the other parent has undermined you with respect to the children and/or made disparaging or negative remarks about you to the children. Additionally, every time you do anything that would show that you are encouraging a good relationship between your children and the other parent, write that down too.

In your journal, first record the date and time that each entry is made. Don't write a novel concerning each incident. Just write a short summary of what happened. Overall, most entries should just be a paragraph or two unless the incident was very serious. When you have a meeting with a lawyer, show him the journal and ask for constructive criticism. A good lawyer should be able to give you advice on how to improve the writing.

Not only will the custody journal give your lawyer some much needed ammunition, but also there are many times that the journal may be admitted into evidence in court. If you are on the stand and are asked a question by your spouse's attorney, you can answer that you are not sure you remember the details of that incident but that, if you can refer to your journal, it would refresh your memory. Assuming that the journal is something that you have been maintaining for a long period of time (not prepared the day before) and that you have been writing down details in it in close proximity to the time the incidents actually happened, many judges will often accept the journal into evidence. A good journal will give you great credibility and strengthen your position beyond a "he said, she said" situation.

There have been many times during a custody trial or hearing that I had my client answer a question with "I don't specifically remember, but if I could please use my journal to refresh my memory, I can answer that." The judge often allowed my client to refer to the journal and as long as it could be shown that the journal was a form of diary that was continuously updated as the incidents occurred, the journal was admitted into evidence.

Getting the entire journal or even a portion of it into the court record can really help you a lot. Keep in mind when you write in the journal that what you write may later be read by a judge and that if it is admitted into evidence, your spouse will also be provided with a copy. Try not to make the entries too long. Just write down enough to let the reader know the facts. Finally, do not put your opinions into your journal. Do not write that your spouse is a "scum-sucking, bottom-feeding liar." Your job is to write down facts about incidents and conversations that happened and allow the reader to reach the desired conclusion by themselves.

Examples of things that should go into your journal include conversations with your spouse about concerns you have about the children during which your spouse is uncooperative, complaints made by the children regarding your spouse, and details of problems or incidents, making sure to write them down as soon as possible after the incidents occur. The bottom line is that, if something happens that bothers you, there should be an entry about it. Be sure to put in the date and time at the beginning of each entry.

Never forget that the judge will be looking to see which parent does more to encourage a relationship with the other parent. Be sure to write down examples of the times that you do this. It is also important that the judge never gets the impression that you are grilling the children for information about the other parent. It is also important that the judge not get the impression that you are doing anything to alienate the children from the other parent.

Finally, remember that your spouse's lawyer may have given him the same advice. Your spouse may even be reading this book! Your spouse may be looking for you to give him or her ammunition in the form of examples of times that you have been destructive to his or her relationship with the children or refused to cooperate in the best interests of the children. Do your best to make sure you don't give your spouse ammunition that can be used against you.

On a final note, the custody journal is something that every competent lawyer should be telling you to maintain if there is even the slightest hint at your initial consultation that there may be issues with custody. If the lawyer does not mention it, I would recommend that you look for a different attorney.

The calendar.

Once you are separated, the second piece of ammunition you need to maintain is a calendar. Find yourself a paper calendar that is at least one-foot square in size. Get a pink highlighter and highlight the dates when your children sleep at your house. This will make a great exhibit in court if you need to establish that the children have already been primarily in your actual custody and a great rebuttal if your spouse tries to claim that the kids are with him almost half the time. For any dates that the children spend time at your home but do not spend the night, highlight those dates with a yellow highlighter and use a pen to write in the time they arrived and the time they left.

The old adage "possession is nine tenths of the law" applies here. When considering custody issues, the judge will take into consideration the history of what the children's routines have been, since less disruption in the children's lives is often in their best interests.

Staying in the Marital Home

The parent who is in the marital home after separation will usually have an advantage when it comes to the initial custody order. The courts often feel that it is in the children's best interest to minimize the disruption in the children's lives as much as possible, so remaining in the home where the children have been living helps a lot. There are three ways in which you can be the one who is in the marital home:

1. The other spouse moves out voluntarily
2. The other spouse is court ordered out of the house through an abuse protection order
3. The courts grant you "exclusive possession" of the marital home and orders your spouse out

An exclusive possession order is available in most states, and, if you need this because the first two options are not available, be sure to discuss this issue with your attorney at the initial consultation.

Procedures

Most often, custody of children is handled one of three ways:

1. The parents don't involve the courts at all and just determine between themselves where the children will live and when they will see the other parent
2. The parents will do what is set forth in number 1 and write it up themselves or have their lawyers write it up
3. The parents are unable to initially come to an agreement and use the court system to resolve custody issues for them.

Parents just having their kids live with one parent and visiting with the other without any written agreement or court order is quite common. The biggest risk with this option is that, if there is a dispute or one parent decides on their own to do something differently or even decides to take the kids and move to another state, there is no system in place that can be easily accessed by the parent who is not happy with the unilateral actions. If the police are called in to intervene, they will not have much authority or ability to do anything, since there is no court order to show them who should legally have the children. I would strongly recommend that any parents following this course of action at least write up their arrangement (see choice two below) and ideally have their agreement incorporated into a court order as set forth in choice three.

An old saying is that an agreement is only as good as the paper it is written on. The point is that it is easy to forget what was agreed to, so with important agreements it's always a good idea to write them down. With custody arrangements, once a verbal agreement is reached, the first thing parents should do is write down the agreement themselves and make at least two originals with dates and both parents' signatures. The advantage of having an agreement written and signed by both parents is that you have come to a meeting of the minds. Even if this is all you have or if the other parent refuses to sign the one drawn up by the lawyer, this first home-made agreement can be used by the court as evidence should you have to go to court to settle a custody dispute. It should be noted that until an agreement is translated into a court order, easy enforcement will not be available.

A better option is to have a lawyer in your state take the home-made agreement and re-write it so that it conforms to your state's laws. Then the lawyer can take the re-written agreement up to a judge and have it made into a court order. Once the agreement becomes a court order, the parents will have several forms of enforcement available if either party fails to comply.

A final option for parents who want a court order to set forth a custodial arrangement or who want to change a prior court order is to petition the court to determine custody for them. This can be done inside a divorce or on its own. Most states will send the parents to a mediator, a parenting coordinator, or a custody master to attempt to settle the matter before it goes to a judge.

We're going to Disney World.

Dan, my client, needed special permission from the custody court to take his two children, ages six and nine, out of state to go to Disney World. The day of the hearing Mom brought the kids to court (they were seated outside) and told the judge that the kids were so afraid of dad that they did not want to go. The judge decided to privately interview the children in his conference room with only the two lawyers present.

The nine-year-old daughter was brought in first and I listened carefully as she told the judge that she did not want to go to Disney World and that she was afraid of her dad. When the judge asked why she was afraid, she answered that she hated his new wife. When the judge asked her why she hated her dad's new wife, she answered that "She doesn't even know how to put on her make-up right." When the judge asked me and the other attorney if we had any questions for the child, we both answered no.

The six-year-old son was brought into the room and mostly repeated what his sister had said. He emphasized that he did not want to go to Disney World because dad and his new wife were mean. When the judge asked him to tell him what his dad does that is "mean," the boy answered that dad yells a lot when he is mad. The judge then asked if the lawyers had any questions, and, thinking to myself that these must be the first two kids in the USA that don't want to go to Disney World, I answered that I would like to ask a couple of questions.

I started by telling the six-year-old that he had done a really, really good job. He smiled from ear to ear. I then asked, "Did you get to practice a lot before you came here today?" The boy, still smiling, nodded yes. I then asked, "Who got to pretend to be the judge when you practiced?" He quickly answered, "Mommy did." I asked, "Who got to be me, your dad's lawyer?" He answered that mom's friend Lester did. I answered "Well, I bet he pretended to be mean, didn't he?" He nodded yes and giggled. Finally, I asked, "The very first time that mommy pretended to be the judge and she asked you if you wanted to go to Disney, did you get the answer wrong?" He looked down and responded that he did. I followed up with, "Did your mommy give you the right answer after that?" and he replied that she did. I noted that both the mom's lawyer and the judge's mouths were agape. I again assured the boy that he had done an excellent job and that he got every answer right. The judge told him he could go out and wait with his sister and mother.

Once the boy was out of the room, I launched into a narrative about the constant parental alienation that had gone on in this case. The mother's lawyer had nothing more to say.

When One Parent Bad-Mouths the Other Parent in Front of the Children

This is also called *disparaging* the other parent. Separation and divorce are such emotionally charged events that one or both parties may experience periods that resemble temporary insanity. Anger and hurt are natural byproducts and having that anger and hurt spill over onto the children happens even when the parents don't want it to or don't do it purposely.

Parents need to understand and remember that children

really do see themselves as half of each of their parents. When one parent infers anything negative at all about the other parent, the children will internalize that. If mom is saying that dad is a bad person in any way, the child will feel that half of them must be bad too. Sadly, many parents fully recognize that they should not disparage or be negative in any way about the other parent, but their anger and hurt is so deep that they do it in front of the children without even being aware of it.

All too common is a situation when this disparagement of the other parent goes on for a period of time well beyond the initial separation period. It often even happens when the parents are together. In both scenarios, the parent doing the disparaging does not even realize how he or she is hurting his or her own children.

Because this problem is so common, judges who try custody cases are very sensitive to this issue, and, as stated before, judges will lean in favor of a parent who truly puts their children's psychological needs first and not only does not disparage the other parent but, for the sake of the children, tries to build up the other parent in the children's eyes.

There is no dispute among the judges and child psychologists involved in custody actions that the best situation for children is one in which (a) parents work together and cooperate when it comes to the kids and (b) the children see their parents as united in a mutual, caring relationship when it comes to their needs. This is the ideal whether the parents are together or apart, and, if this is not happening, the judges will try to place the children with the parent who most tries to make it happen.

It is critical to remember that, if a case ends up in front of a custody judge, the judge will assume right at the outset that one or both of the parents are incapable of putting their children's needs first; otherwise, the case would never have made its way to court. Judges assume that if both parents could put their children's needs first, they would not be putting the decisions as to what is best for them in the hands of a stranger, i.e., the judge. So, the judge will see one of his primary responsibilities as determining which parent is more at fault for not doing what is best for the kids. Which parent is more likely to encourage a good relationship between the kids and the other parent and which parent is really not understanding that his or her disparaging the other parent hurts the children?

Your lawyer's job in a custody case is to convince the judge that the custody arrangement you want is what will be best for your children, that you do not say negative things about the other parent in front of the kids, and that you do your best to work with and cooperate with the other parent for the sake of the kids. Your lawyer will also need to convince the judge that, if there are problems of parental non-cooperation and parental disparagement, they are primarily with the other parent and not you. You will need to provide your lawyer with all the information and ammunition to support these positions.

The rocks in one head match the holes in the other.
(Divorce lawyers discussing their clients and their clients' spouses)

It is the natural inclination of those in and out of the legal system to assume that *both* parents are equally at fault when it comes to problems relating to the children or the inability of parents to cooperate for the sake of their children. In my experience, sometimes this is true, but, more often, one parent carries far more blame for the couple's inability to do what's best for their kids. One parent may be letting anger cloud his or her judgment to the point that he or she is using the children as a weapon to hurt and retaliate against the other parent. One parent may just not have great common sense or the intuition to understand what is best for the children or one parent may have emotional or mental problems that spill over onto the children. The list of possibilities goes on and on.

A good lawyer's job is to realize that the judge will naturally assume that all problems and conflicts are equally both parents' fault, and, if that is not the case, the lawyer's job is to move the judge's initial perception of equal fault to what the actual dynamics of the specific case are. The custody client needs to be aware of this goal and provide his or her lawyer with the information needed to convince the judge that the best interests of the children will be better served with him or her, assuming that is the case.

One of the most common tactics used by the man's lawyer is to portray the mother as someone who is overly emotional to the extent that she is consumed with irrational anger and that she is purposely alienating the children from him as a form of retaliation. This portrayal serves him by diminishing her credibility when she describes problems and incidents relating to the father and by helping to bolster his claim that the children are better off with him, since he is "far more stable." Unfortunately, this tactic is often used because it works; it plays into stereotypes that the judges have seen played out many times, so that it is often an effective strategy even when it should not be.

Women are taught at a very young age that it is ok to express their emotions, while men are often taught to hide or bury them. A marriage that is breaking up is by its very nature emotionally charged, so women need to be aware that their expressions of strong emotional turmoil can and will often be used against them in a custody dispute. Part of a good custody lawyer's job will be to do everything possible not to let his client be perceived as emotionally irrational. The lawyer should make sure the client fully understands this tactic. He or she should structure the client's testimony and statements so that they are not full of opinions and conclusions but instead focus on details of incidents that would lead the judge to the desired opinion. This does not mean that a mother should never cry or express emotion to the court. Instead, crying and other expressions of emotion should accompany descriptions of events that any rational person would find especially distressing. Less is more here. While testifying to a judge, a woman needs to be clinically detailed for the most part while simultaneously making sure the judge feels her love and concern for her children.

Another common tactic is that the father and his lawyer will portray the mother as emotionally attached to the children to an unstable degree. The father or his lawyer will claim that the mother can't bear to be separated from the children and that she is "helicoptering" into their lives by constantly calling them when they are with the father. The father will claim that this unhealthy attachment to the children is the basis for her "delusional" aspersions against him and that her statements should not be given any credibility. Along these lines, the father may also claim that the mother is constantly interrogating the children about what they do when they are with their dad, implying to the children that the father is acting inappropriately with them.

The mother's lawyer needs to make her aware of this tactic so that she does not provide the father with ammunition that supports it. Here again, a detailed journal that not only documents the children's statements but also explains the circumstances surrounding why and when the children made the statements is useful. The mother should avoid calling her children when they are with their father, but, at the same time, she should make it clear to them that they are welcome to call her whenever they feel like it. When the mother talks to her children during the time they are with father, a journal entry should be made that specifically states who initiated the call. Additionally, when the children are in the mother's household, they should be free to call their father whenever they want, but, if possible, the mother should make journal entries detailing when these calls are made to demonstrate that the children are comfortable calling their dad while they are with her, and thus she is encouraging the relationship with their father. Many clients will have a separate section of their journal that is dedicated to listing calls from and to the children, noting which parent they are calling and which household they are making the calls from.

Drug and Alcohol Abuse Issues

Too close for comfort.
A third of my work came from other lawyers; they rarely sent me the easy cases. A mother of a three-year-old little girl came into my office one day after being referred by another attorney. Mom had a master's degree in mathematics and held a responsible position with a good company. While high on cocaine, mom sideswiped a mailbox at high speed. Her daughter was in a car seat behind her, and the little girl was covered with broken glass from the car's window right next to the child seat. Mom then fled the scene on foot, abandoning the child. Dad was now seeking full custody, and mom wanted to hire me to keep that from happening.

Mom shared with me that she had been working on her addiction with a series of professionals and that she was now "clean." Her drug abuse was reportedly a thing of the past. She even provided me with a letter from her psychologist saying she was in full recovery.

At the first court status meeting, I met her ex-husband, a very clean cut, young man who was employed by a very respectable company as a chemical engineer. He made it clear that he did not trust that my client would not go back to using drugs, and he wanted full custody. The judge ordered a 2nd status conference to hear presentations by the attorneys and their clients as to what sort of investigations the court should pursue.

About a week before my client was scheduled to show up for her 2nd status conference before the court, I got a call that she had relapsed with cocaine, had checked herself into an inpatient rehabilitation hospital, and would not be able to make the court hearing. That same day, I received a notice from the Federal Court that a hearing had been scheduled for a different case involving a child that had been removed from the country. Since Federal hearings must be given preference by the state courts, the custody status hearing was continued (delayed) for a month… Some people are just born lucky.

Apparently, neither the ex-husband nor his attorney found out about my client's relapse. At the rescheduled 2nd status conference, the court ordered an independent, court-appointed psychologist to evaluate the parties and talk to my client's counselors. The final recommendation was a shared custody arrangement with a biweekly drug test for a year. My client was happy not to totally lose custody of her daughter, and I made sure that she knew what would happen if she were to come back to court because of drugs ever again. If there ever was another problem, I never heard about it.

Unfortunately, drug and alcohol abuse issues are one of the most common reasons for parents not staying together. Another sad fact is that, with these types of issues, the parent with the problem is usually in denial about both the existence of the substance use disorder and how the problem is affecting their children. The parent who will be raising these issues about the other parent will have to be able to educate the court as to the extent of the other parent's problem and detail examples about how these problems have affected their children.

Most custody courts/judges are very familiar with these issues and often have the power to get other experts involved to determine the extent of the substance use disorder. I have seen a judge order both parents, right in their courtroom, to go directly from the courtroom to have drug tests done. I have also seen many court orders for regular drug testing as a condition for visitation. Rehabilitation and other forms of treatments are often court ordered as a condition for interaction with children.

Explosive Tempers and Physical Abuse

A full separate chapter in this book deals with both child abuse and spousal abuse. If you feel this is an issue in your case, please read it carefully and make sure that you have made your lawyer aware of the abuse history.

Relocation

I have heard many judges when confronted with a relocation request say, "Well, we are a mobile society." That being said, when a parent who has primary physical custody or equal shared custody wants to move far enough away that the other parent's visitation or time with the children will need to be changed, and, if the parents cannot come to a new agreement themselves, a request to the courts will have to be made to change the custodial arrangement.

The parent wanting to make the move will have an uphill climb or otherwise known as the legal burden to show that the move is for what the court considers a legitimate reason. If a judge gets the impression that you are seeking to move just to get away from the other parent or to make a fresh start, the court may decide that, if you do move, you cannot keep primary or equal shared custody. Moving because you (or your new/current spouse) have a better employment opportunity is the most common scenario. Moving to be closer to extended family who can offer a better support system is also common.

The court's options when confronted with a relocation request is to allow the move and change the other parent's schedule of time with the children or deny the move, which means that the other parent may gain primary custody and there will be a new visitation schedule. The new schedules for the non-moving parent when the move is allowed generally will be that the children will go back to the non-moving parent for the majority of the summer (usually they will give the moving parent a couple of weeks for their summer vacation) and the majority of the other school breaks like Christmas and spring breaks. The court will also often determine who will be responsible for the costs of the children's transportation, sometimes splitting it and sometimes making the moving parent pay for all of it.

If you are planning or would like to move, it is important that you be able to set forth in as much detail as possible why the move will benefit you and in turn the children. A new job with more money and better housing and schools are often brought up. Be sure to be able to explain how you have done a lot of research on your new proposed area, even having visited possible houses and potential schools for your children.

The judge will have to balance the benefits of the move against the downside to the other parent of not seeing the children as frequently as he or she would like or as frequently as in the past. It will be important for your lawyer to prove that your motives for the move are honorable and not frivolous. Your lawyer should also be emphasizing that modern technology like Facetime, WhatsApp, and Skype video calls have made it a lot easier for the non-moving parent to maintain frequent face to face contact with the children and that he or she will be able to continue to foster the relationship and stay involved with the children.

Most of the time, if the judge denies the request for the move, the judge will give the parent who is requesting the move the choice of keeping the schedule the same as it has been in the past and forgoing the move. As such, most of the time, the only downside to petitioning for the right to move and modify the other parents schedule is the legal costs of the court action. Many states also have an expedited or faster system to deal with relocation petitions since they are aware that time is often short.

I have often been asked by parents who have the kids with them most of the time (primary custody), "What if I just go?" If there is no existing court order in place and if the other parent is notified about the move and given all the details as to the addresses and phone numbers where the children will be and a new visitation schedule is proposed, this is legal. There are two sides to this course of action that must be considered. The upside is that if the other parent does not take any legal action, once you have been with the children at your new residence for a set period of time (six months in many states), the jurisdiction will shift to your new area/state, and, if the parent left behind did not object to the courts at the time of the move, the courts could determine that they were at least initially in agreement to the move. The downside is that, if the parent who is left behind acts quickly and files a legal action with the court at your old residential area, you may have to travel back there for court hearings and the court could order that you either return with the children or turn primary custody over to the other parent.

If a court order for custody already exists or if you know the other parent will probably take immediate legal action if you just move without their approval, then the proper action would be for you to have your attorney file a petition asking the court to allow the move and set up the new schedules before you go.

The Other Parent Has Mental Health Problems

This claim comes up a lot in custody cases. If you feel mental health is an issue with your children's other parent, it is important to provide a lot of detail to your lawyer in the summary of background information you prepare. Put down details of actions and incidents that have occurred that lead you to this belief. If the other parent is being treated for mental health issues by a physician, psychiatrist, or psychologist and if they have been prescribed any drugs for mental issues, your lawyer needs to know about this. If you feel that the other parent is self-medicating in any way for a mental health issue, this information also needs to be shared with your attorney. Of course, if there have been any times that you felt the children were negatively impacted because of the other parent's mental health issues, these should be detailed for your lawyer as well. Finally, if there is any history of mental health issues in the other parent's family, your lawyer should also be made aware of this.

One of the options that will be available to your lawyer in most states is to request that the court appoint an independent psychologist to evaluate both parents. This psychologist will not act as a counselor but instead will usually perform a series of psychological tests on both parents and possibly the children. He/she will also interview both parents, and he or she may also see and talk to the children. Often, your lawyer will advise you to share and discuss with the evaluating psychologist the issues you listed and detailed in the summary of background information that you originally prepared for your lawyer.

Before requesting the court-appointed independent psychologist, it is important to realize that the judges will often put great weight on the psychologist's final report and recommendations. The judges value these reports because they are considered independent and thus not a witness for either side, and, although the report could end up recommending against you being the primary custodian of your children, if there are serious mental issues at play with your spouse, this may be the route your lawyer recommends.

Many times, the primary reason an independent, court-appointed psychologist is not used relates to the cost and the inability to afford it. The easiest way to get an independent psychologist appointed is to offer to pay all the costs. In some states, the option is only available if the person requesting it pays for it. In many other states the cost is equally split and in some states the cost is divided proportional with the parties' incomes. A lawyer who is experienced with custody matters should be able to tell you the approximate cost and the likelihood of the court granting a request to have one appointed. The lawyer should also be able to tell you the court's standard practice as to how the costs are generally divided.

A New Significant Other

Once you have separated, no one expects you or the other parent to join a convent or monastery, so it's probably just a matter of time until both you and the other parent become involved with other people. The most important thing to remember is that the custody courts will evaluate everyone that will have significant exposure to your children. As such, if there is a custody dispute, not only will you and your actions be put under a microscope but any person that will be regularly exposed to your children may go under the same microscope. Bottom line is that you will be judged by the company you keep.

It is natural to be angry and jealous of the other parent's new love interest. Yet, assuming the worst about this new person in your children's lives, acting hostile, and saying negative things about this new person will not serve you well if a custody battle ensues. Remember, your children are human sponges, and they will reflect your attitude. Being negative, acting jealous, and showing your anger will harm your children in the long run by harming their relationship with their other parent. Behave improperly in this situation, and it can be used against you later. At the same time, if the other parent is being negative, acting jealous, and showing anger to your new significant other, you should detail it in your background summary and journal.

With children come responsibilities and who you or the other parent expose your children to will provide evidence of your good judgment or lack thereof. If you are considering getting involved with anyone, you will need to thoroughly check them out. Background checks are easily available on the internet. Never assume anyone is a good or nice person just because they seem that way. You may be called up to detail and explain what actions you took to check out anyone you exposed your children to and the failure to do this can easily be held against you. Also, there is nothing wrong with doing a thorough check of the person the other parent has brought into the children's lives.

This situation is one where it will serve your children well if you let go of the anger and jealousy and do your best to get along, not only with your children's other parent but with anyone that is especially important to them. Often you will find that being friendly to that person can help you a lot in the long run. Since they are not as close to the emotional fire, they may be able to serve as a calmer voice that can help you with issues that arise. Don't fall into the destructive trap of comparing yourself to the significant other or wondering what they have that you don't. Everyone has good and bad traits. Work to find the good and positive in this situation, and you will have a better chance of helping your children.

Of course, if there are any substantial problems or issues with the other parent's significant other, you will need to take action to protect your children. Discuss the issues with your lawyer to find out what remedies are available.

Communicating with the Court-Appointed Independent Evaluator

Most often, the evaluator who will eventually write a report and possibly testify in court will interview the parents first. Your job is to make sure the evaluator has a full understanding of the situation from your perspective. My advice would be that you prepare an outline of the areas you want to cover in your interview. In that outline, I would suggest you not write out everything you want to say but, instead, make a list of key points that you can refer to as you talk, so that you can mentally check off each area and then fill in the information and background from memory.

I would suggest that the outline include the following main subjects:

1. History and background. Here you will talk about how long you have been married, your and your spouse's work history, the ages and general information about each child, and what the custody arrangements have been to date.

2. The problems. Talk about the issues and problems regarding your spouse that you believe have an impact on your children.

3. Your proposed/desired custodial arrangement. Explain your desired proposal for custody and visitation and why you think your proposal would be best for your children. Remember, that what both the evaluator *and* the judge will be considering is what is best for your children. One of the biggest factors they will consider is which parent is most likely to try and foster a good relationship with the other parent. Be sure to talk about what you have done and what you will do in the future to foster this consideration.

4. History. The other big factor that the evaluators and judges will consider when it comes to parenting is the history. Be sure to point out how you have been the parent who has had the primary responsibility when it comes to dealing with your children's doctors, teachers, and extracurricular activities.

Unless the children are very young, there is a high probability that the evaluator will be talking to the children. Here it is important that the evaluator never get the impression that you have "coached" the children or have tried to put words in their mouths. Most evaluators have been trained to spot coaching and most will hold it against the parent who they think did this. The kids should only be told that it is important that they tell the truth.

How to Behave in Court

Custody judges assume that parents will lie for the sake of their children and therefore, all parents in custody court are probably lying or at the very least, exaggerating and embellishing when they are testifying. So, if you are expecting to be believed in custody court, you have an uphill climb.

The first rule of thumb is to avoid giving opinions and judgments if possible. The judges see this as their job not yours. Instead, try to be precise and give as many details that will lead the judge to have the same opinion you do. The more details and examples of actions and statements made by the other parent that there are to support your opinion, the better. Stay focused on each incident before starting on a different incident. Whenever possible, if there is someone else who heard or witnessed the actions or behaviors, you will want them to testify and support your story. The more removed they are from your direct family, the more validity the judge will give to their descriptions. Of course, tape recordings can help to verify your version of events but there are many rules as to when they can or can't be used in court. You may even be committing a crime by recording someone who does not know they are being recorded, so be sure to clear the use and circumstances of the recorder with your lawyer. Messages left on answering devices and voice mails are almost always allowed and admitted because it is common knowledge that when you leave a message you are being recorded. So, if the other parent or anyone leaves a message on your voicemail that supports your description of events, be sure to capture or re-record said message to save it for later use.

Try to remain calm when you are testifying but do not be afraid to show some human emotion when describing things that would upset the average person. Listen to questions carefully and think before you answer. Remember, it is the other lawyer's job to try to get you upset so that you are not thinking clearly when you answer. Don't fall for it. Don't become belligerent or try to out-argue a lawyer; that is your lawyer's job, not yours. If you answer questions calmly (for the most part) and precisely with a lot of relevant detail, you will help your case, and when the other parent's lawyer questions you, it will not be as long if he feels your answers are hurting and not helping his case.

Try to remember and describe as much detail as possible when answering questions, but if you are asked a very specific detail that the average person would not remember it is OK to mention that the specific answer to the question you are being asked is in your journal and you can answer if given a chance to look at your journal to refresh your memory. Just remember that if you look at it, the judge and your spouse's lawyer will have the right to see it too. There is nothing wrong with letting them see your journal as long as you kept this possibility in mind when you wrote the entries.

When you are asked a question, be sure to pause for a few seconds. The benefits of doing this are that you are more likely to answer properly if you took a few seconds to think before you speak. This will also give your attorney time to object if the question is improper. When you do hear a question be sure to stop talking until the objection is resolved and you are directed that it is OK to answer.

Too often the better liar wins in court. When I first started practicing law and I was more passionate and idealistic, an older, far more experienced lawyer warned me that a courtroom is not the best place to be looking for truth and justice. For this very reason, it has often been said that even a bad settlement is often better than a good lawsuit. The reality is that there are frequently times when there are no other options available than to go to court and pray for the best.

A good lawyer will prepare you for court by explaining the points made here and providing many more. If the lawyer has never seen you on the stand, the lawyer should do a short practice run, asking you some of the questions they will be asking you in court and even pretending to be your spouse's lawyer, asking you some questions from their point of view. The lawyer will not be trying to have you rehearse your answers as this may make you less credible. Instead, the lawyer will often do this to evaluate your demeanor and to see if you are following the instructions he gave you. Your lawyer will often have a practice run to help him or her form his or her own opinion as to how credible you are on the stand.

If you think the other parent is just a great liar and that you will have problems in court, it may be a good idea to request a court appointed psychologist. These professionals are often highly experienced, and their opinions are well regarded and given great weight by the court. A good psychologist will do evaluations that are far more thorough and be able to go far deeper than a judge will be able to do in a courtroom. The downside is that, of course, there are no guarantees that they will find the truth as you know it and the appointment will often be costly.

Grandparents' and Stepparents' Rights

In most states there are no grandparent or stepparents' custody rights, but there may be exceptions. If this is a concern, you should discuss it further with your lawyer. If your children have a history of a relationship with a grandparent or stepparent that you believe is not harmful, you should be prepared to discuss the history of the relationship, why it is beneficial to the child/children, and how you intend to continue to foster it.

5

Support

Show Me the Money.
Larry Miller was a minister whose wife, my client, had left, taking
their five children with her. Of course, he did not feel her reasons
for leaving were valid but that is another story. During the support
conference before the hearing master, Reverend Miller, upon
hearing the amount of money he would be required to pay in
support, dropped to his knees and with both arms extended to the
heavens exclaimed, "Lord, I will go to jail before I pay that
woman any money!" I replied, "You know, there are a lot of men
at that jail who I think will benefit greatly from your services and
hearing the word of God; let me see what I can do to make that
happen."

I am sad to say that when Reverend Miller received his support
order he complied and paid, so he never saw the inside of a jail cell.
Seems to me that when someone makes a deal with God, they
should follow through with that deal, especially when that someone
is a minister.

Getting Ready

Remember, lawyers sell their time. The more you can do yourself, the less the lawyer will cost you. When it comes to child support, spousal support, and pre- and post-divorce alimony the most important consideration that you will need is accurate information as to what you and your spouse make in income per month. Of course, you have easy access to your own information, so your focus will be on obtaining documentation showing your spouse's income. If you filed joint tax returns with your spouse, you should be able to provide your lawyer with copies of those returns for at least the last three years. If you don't have them, contact the closest IRS office and get copies. This can often be done on-line, and, as long as your name is on them, they are available to you. Copies of your spouse's pay stubs and copies of all bank and financial statements for the last few years can also be important, especially if you do not believe your spouse is showing all the income or he is self-employed or owns his own company. Do not despair if you are unable to get these as this is something a lawyer can easily do; however, whatever information you can provide about funds to which your spouse has access will be beneficial.

Is a Court Order Really Necessary?

"My spouse is already paying the bills and giving me money; do I really need a court order for support?" This question is important, and it comes up a lot. Many men who earn far more than their wives don't ignore the obligation to support their family and voluntarily keep paying the bills and giving their spouses money to live on so the *dependent spouse* must make the decision whether to just leave things alone or file for a formal court support order. This issue is one that a competent family law lawyer should be exploring at the initial consultation.

The reality is that, in some states, it can take as little as a few weeks to get a support order, while in other states the process can take months. Many times, the lawyer may determine that the client is getting more money directly and in the form of bill payments than the court would order. In these situations, the lawyer may advise the client to file only if the spouse who is paying stops. The risk is that if the paying spouse stops giving money voluntarily, there could be a period of time the client will have to go without support waiting for a court order.

The big advantage of court ordered support is that there are always methods of *enforcement* that come along with the court order. The paying spouse's wages can be attached, and their employer can be ordered to deduct the support from their paycheck. The paying spouse can also be brought into court for being in *contempt*, and, in almost every state, the court does have the power to put a spouse in jail for failing to pay.

If your lawyer does determine that you are getting more from your spouse than the court would order them to pay, the ideal would be to try to get an *agreed order* where both you and your spouse sign a document laying out the support obligation he is paying and further agreeing that this can be incorporated into a court order. Many times though, getting an agreement as to support in writing is not feasible as the client may determine that even trying for one might upset their spouse and cause him to cut off the support or reduce the amount. In these cases, it may often be the best course to just do nothing and only take action to get court ordered support if and when the paying spouse stops making the payments. The key here is that if you are in this situation you should be educated by your lawyer as to how long you are likely to go without the money until the court can put you through the process. You should also know exactly what actions you need to take to start the process of getting court ordered support.

Getting Support Fast

If you and your spouse cannot reach an agreement before or immediately after separation, in almost every state there is a court procedure where your lawyer can seek a *temporary order* or an *emergency support order* setting up an amount of support to be paid while the court moves forward with the procedures to set a long term support order. Frequently, this order will be less than the final order but at least it will get money flowing sooner rather than later.

Calculating Child Support

If the children live with one parent more than the other, child support will be awarded to the parent who has the children more than the other. The court will often go by where the children sleep so if they spend more overnights per month with one parent that parent will be able to get child support. A parent who has the kids exactly half the time may also be able to get child support but that will be discussed later.

The procedure to apply and receive support is slightly different from state to state, but the procedure used in your state is something that every family law attorney should be able to explain. Additionally, the procedure to sign up for child support for most states and counties can be found on-line. Once you are not under the same roof as the other parent, it becomes important to sign up as soon as possible, since the other parent will not owe any support for the period of time before you signed up but will owe back support to the date you signed up.

If the other parent is paying the bills and giving you money to support the children, you should still consult with a lawyer to find out if the amount of money you are getting is at least what you would get through the court system. In almost every state, the courts upon request will send a court order for support to the other parents' employer requiring that the money be a payroll deduction that will automatically be sent to you.

Almost every state uses what are known as *guidelines* to set the amount of money you should get as child support. These guidelines are primarily based on each parent's after-tax income but other factors like mortgages and health insurance costs may also be considered in many states. If you can provide a family law attorney with the approximate amount both you and the other parent make each month after taxes, the lawyer should be able to give you an approximation as to how much you will probably get in child support.

It is important to also understand that although most states will require that you and the other parent fill out a form detailing all your expenses, these expenses are often not given a lot of weight since the courts do not want to penalize a parent who is frugal or reward a parent who spends a lot. By the same token, the parent who will be paying support may not get much consideration for the expenses and bills they have since the courts feel that the children's needs must come first.

Support Procedures

As stated previously, if you as a custodial parent are not getting enough or any money from the other parent, it is important to sign up for support as soon as possible. In most states this is not something you need a lawyer to do for you. Research signing up for child support in your county on the internet and go in and fill out the forms.

After you have signed up for child support (and possibly spousal support or pre-divorce alimony as will be discussed a little later) the next step does vary some from state to state. Usually, a hearing will be scheduled with some form of hearing officer or mediator. That non-judge will usually apply the state guidelines and propose the amount set forth in the guidelines. In many states, if there is no agreement to that amount, an order will be entered for the guideline amount with the right of appeal to a judge. In other states, if no agreement is reached, the matter is then scheduled to a judge who will enter an order for support. The order will go back retroactively to the date you signed up for support and the back amounts due will often be known as arrearages and an amount to reduce the arrearages will be added to the support amount you will get. Often in the first hearing the paying parent's lawyer will try to get as part of an agreement the waiver or forgiveness of the back support (the arrears). I would never recommend doing this as this is asking for something a judge will never do. Any amounts paid to you by the non-custodial parent between the date you signed up and the date of the order will be credited against any possible arrears they owe.

The paying parent's lawyer may also try to get you to agree to an amount that is less than the state guideline. Here again, I would never advise a client to agree to this as it is very rare for a judge to deviate from the guidelines.

If a support order is appealed or a hearing officer's or mediator's recommended amount is not agreed to, the support case may then proceed to a judge. Very few cases actually end up going this far, because in most states it is very rare for a judge to deviate from the guideline amount, so going to the judge is often a waste of time and lawyers' fees. Cases that end up in front of judges are more often those in which a parent is self-employed or works for their own company and there is likelihood that all their income is not being reported. This issue will be discussed later in this chapter.

The amount of time it takes to go from signing up for support and getting a court order also varies greatly by state. The more progressive states do their best to shorten this time period. Your lawyer should be able to give you an accurate estimate as to how long the procedure will take. If you do not have the income or savings to cover your expenses while waiting for a final order, the other lawyer may try to take advantage of you by having you waive your back support in exchange for a faster order. Some states do have a procedure for a quick emergency hearing to get some support going if you are in desperate need. This is also something to discuss with your lawyer.

It is important to remember that, even if you as the custodial parent make more money than the non-custodial parent, they will still be required to pay support, since both parents have a legal obligation to support their children regardless of their income. The fact that you make more simply means that you will get a little less in support than you would have if you made less.

"What if I Don't Want Child Support?"

There are two reasons most often given by a parent who tells me they do not want child support. The most common is that the parent saying this does not want the other parent involved with the child's life and think that if they go for support that this will just drive the other parent to seek more visitation. Here it is important to understand that, in almost every state, issues of child support and custody/visitation are handled by totally separate procedures and laws. Legally one has nothing to do with the other. A custodial parent does not have the legal right to deny visitation if there are no other problems (like drug use or abuse), even if they are not getting any money for support. At the same time, a non-custodial parent who is paying support is *not* automatically entitled to see the child. If one of these concerns is raised, support judges and officials will tell the parent that custody and visitation are not handled at the same time and that they have different procedures, laws and rules.

The second reason most commonly given by a custodial parent who denies wanting support is that they don't need the money and don't want to place a financial burden on the non-custodial parent. I have often explained to those clients who tell me this that their non-action in seeking support can actually be held against them, since these funds, regardless of how much money they may have, could be used to better the child's life and that their not seeking the support could be deemed to be hurting their child. Even if the custodial parent does not think their child lacks for anything at present, the support funds could be saved for use in the future, for example, placed into a college fund.

Consider the following illustration of a cross examination related to child support that could occur in court:

("FL" = father's lawyer and "M" = mother)

> FL: *Isn't it a fact that you never signed up for child support?*
> M: *Yes, I didn't need it.*
> FL: *Isn't it also a fact that when the child's father sent you checks you never cashed them?*
> M: *Yes, like I said, I didn't need them, and I didn't want anything from him.*
> FL: *If you had gotten more money, would you have spent it on yourself or the child?*
> M: *On the child of course.*
> FL: *So, you acknowledge that you could have done more for this child but put your needs and your anger towards the child's father ahead of the child's needs.*

Support with Shared or Equal Time Custody

If you have a custodial arrangement in which the kids are spending equal time at both homes, this does not mean that you are not going to be able to get child support. If the other parent has a higher income, then in most states you can still get support. Often, it will simply be less than you would have received were the children sleeping at your residence more nights than at the other parent's home.

Spousal Support/Pre-Divorce Alimony and Post-Divorce Alimony

Swimming in the sewers.
I will never forget sitting at a spousal support hearing with my
client, the 2nd wife of a corporate jet pilot. The husband's lawyer
immediately stated that he was contesting her entitlement to
spousal support, because she had reportedly committed marital
misconduct in the form of adultery. My client leaned over and
whispered to me that she would like to talk to me privately, so I
asked to step outside with her. Once we were outside the room, my
client told me that she had never cheated but that she strongly
suspected that her husband was having an affair. Then she went
on to tell me that, in her safety deposit box at her bank, she had a
small mirror that her husband used to snort cocaine. She was sure
that the mirror would have traces of cocaine and his fingerprints on
it.

We walked back into the hearing room, and I asked to speak to
the husband's attorney privately. When we were out of the room, I
repeated what my client had told me about the cocaine mirror in
her safety deposit box. I could see all the blood drain from both the
husband's and his lawyer's faces. The lawyer walked his client
outside to speak with him privately. When he returned, we took
15 minutes and settled the entire divorce case, with very favorable
terms for my client I might add. No wonder so many lawyers say
divorce law is like swimming in a sewer.

It is important to understand that there are different types of support that may be available to you if your spouse makes more money than you do. These include spousal support, pre-divorce alimony, and post-divorce alimony.

If your spouse has a much higher income than you do, in many states you may be able to get spousal support money whether you have kids or not, as this type of support is separate and can be awarded in addition to child support, whether or not you have any kids in common. In most states, you must be legally married to get this type of support though.

Spousal support often does not require that a divorce be filed. As long as you are not residing in the same house as your spouse and your spouse makes more than you do, you may want to consider requesting spousal support. Here again, any support you get will only go back to the date you signed up, so the sooner you do this the better. If you are not living under the same roof but your spouse is voluntarily paying the household bills, you should review your situation with a family law attorney to see if you would receive more through the court system. The other advantage of getting your support through the courts is that you would have recourse should your spouse stop giving you money or stop paying the bills.

With spousal support many states require you to be the "innocent and injured spouse." This means that if you moved out without good cause or if you are living with a paramour, you may not get spousal support. Often, no divorce action is required to get spousal support, and, in many states, you can sign up for this type of support without even having an attorney.

Pre-divorce alimony is also available in most states if your spouse makes more than you do. This type of support is generally only available after a divorce action has been filed. It usually makes no difference who filed for the divorce. The big advantage to this type of support is that in most states you can get this type of support regardless of fault. This means that issues of who left whom and why do not matter. Generally, pre-divorce alimony will require an attorney as it is a claim that is usually filed within a divorce action.

Post-divorce alimony is support for a spouse that is paid by a higher earning spouse after a final divorce. This must be awarded as part of the divorce, and often there are more requirements that must be met to get it when compared to spousal support (support while you are still married but not living together) and pre-divorce alimony. The biggest factor that courts in most states consider when determining whether to award post-divorce alimony is the length of the marriage. There are also many other factors that the courts take into consideration with post-divorce alimony, but this is an area that should be discussed with your attorney. Post-divorce alimony can be for life or it can be for a set period of time. The length of the marriage and other factors which your lawyer can explain are used by the court to determine the length of time for the alimony award.

Post-divorce alimony will often contain a provision that it will end immediately upon the remarriage of the spouse who is receiving it. It can also end if the receiving spouse starts living with a paramour. If you/your lawyer are negotiating a settlement, you may also be able to try to get an agreement that the alimony will not end upon remarriage or cohabitation. In a settlement, you should also insist that your spouse obtain or continue life insurance that names you as beneficiary in an amount that would cover both child support and alimony. Post-divorce alimony will be further discussed later in this book.

How to Find Hidden Income

Remember, the court is generally using guidelines to determine how much child or spousal support or alimony your spouse should be paying. The guideline system requires that your income and your spouse's income be used to set the amount. If your spouse is claiming a lower income than they are really getting and this lower number is used by the court, your support order will be less than you are entitled to.

When your spouse is self-employed or has income from any source other than a regular full-time job, you will want a lawyer who has experience in this area. Typically, the court will only obtain your spouse's last tax return and copies of his pay stubs to determine his income for support purposes. Your lawyer should be seeking copies of at least a year's worth of financial statements (both personal and corporate) for any account your spouse has an interest in. In more complex cases with higher income earners you may also want to hire what is known as a forensic accountant. A good domestic law attorney should know several to recommend.

Once the bank and financial institution statements have been obtained, the first step is to add up all the deposits made in a tax year and compare this amount to the total income claimed on the tax return. A good lawyer will put the burden on your spouse to explain any discrepancy by making the spouse prove the reason for any deposits not included in the tax return.

The next step is to review and add up all amounts spent. It is not unusual to find that the total of the amounts spent is higher than the amount your spouse is claiming as his income. Here again, your lawyer should be requiring your spouse to explain in detail why the amount he is spending is higher than his income and where he is getting the money to do that. If your spouse cannot show proof of loans to explain the difference this can often be deemed evidence that your spouse is not reporting all his income to the IRS.

Although a forensic accountant who takes the time to really review several years of financial records may get lucky and trace a debit, often there will be no paper trail, as your spouse had the funds deposited directly to the hidden account from the source. Another thing a forensic accountant and your attorney can do is focus on any major purchases and require that your spouse provide the paper trail for all funds used in those purchases.

Finally, if your spouse has applied for any loans, it would be a good idea to have your attorney use the court's discovery powers, like subpoenas, to compel the financial institution who provided the loan to provide a copy of your spouse's loan application. Many times your spouse will use his actual earnings or he may even have inflated his earnings in his effort to secure the loan. Lying on a loan application is a criminal offense (bank fraud) and many judges will use the declared earnings on the loan application rather than a tax return's stated earnings.

Cash earners.

Many times, a spouse who is claiming a lower income for support purposes is not showing all his income to the IRS because he is getting cash rather than checks for compensation. The best method to prove this to the court is for you to list all amounts he generally spends on regular expenses, both household and personal that you know about. Add this total monthly amount to the fact that he is not taking out loans or racking up credit cards, and your claim that he gets cash income will be given more weight. Often in this type of situation your word alone about the amount he is actually earning in cash will be taken by the court as evidence, since the courts do not look kindly on cheating the IRS and will often go with the amount you state he is earning despite his claim that it's not that much.

Besides listing all the regular expenses your spouse pays, as described above, it is also a good idea to list all major purchases that you know or believe your spouse bought with cash, like cars, boats, tools, etc. Additionally, if your spouse has been romantically involved with someone else, you may want to have your lawyer require that person to appear for a deposition during which they will have to answer under oath what your spouse has spent on them in the form of gifts, dinners out, etc.

You may never find the money your spouse has hidden.

Many times, your spouse has planned his exit from the marriage for a long time and has been taking actions to hide accounts and income long before you were clued into what was going on. As described above, you/your lawyer can try to work backwards by showing the court that money is being hidden because your spouse's expenses exceed what they are claiming they earn.

As discussed more fully in the section of this book dealing with property division, your lawyer will have what are known as "discovery tools" that allow him to issue subpoenas and take depositions where people can be questioned under oath before a court reporter. If you think there is a possibility that your spouse has hidden income or assets, it is critical that a complete record be made so that if it is later discovered that your spouse failed to make a full disclosure, your case can be reopened.

It is important to ask your lawyer to detail what he or she will do to find these funds or assets and then further explain how they will make sure that if the funds or assets are later found your claim will be kept alive or *preserved*.

I think we're done here.

We were near the end of the support conference that had gone on for over an hour. Suddenly, my client's husband, who was there without an attorney, turned to me and yelled at the top of his lungs, "I KNOW YOU ARE F**KING MY WIFE."

Stunned, I replied, "I think we are done here," and my client and I left the room. Outside, my mortified client kept apologizing for her husband. I assured her that "it was no big deal," said goodbye and headed back to my office. I was not at my desk for more than 5 minutes when my receptionist called me over the intercom to inform me that my client's husband was in my waiting room asking to speak to me. Unsure about his intentions, I opened my desk drawer and took out the loaded handgun that I kept there, slipped it into my pocket, and walked out to see what he wanted. When I walked into my waiting room, my client's husband was standing there sobbing. He turned to me and apologized repeatedly, saying that he had jumped to the conclusion that his wife was having sex with me because of the way I was fighting for her so passionately. I assured him that I was not having sex with his wife and that I was a happily married man with three young children. For years after that incident, my client's husband referred clients to my law firm, telling them that I was the best lawyer he had ever seen in action.

6

Divorce

The skeletons in the closet will emerge.
I had filed a divorce and a claim for visitation for Bill about two
weeks earlier when I received a call from him. He told me that he
had been arrested by the military police and was in custody at a
Naval Base in Philadelphia. He then proceeded to tell me the
back story. Bill, who had been married for 10 years to his high
school sweetheart Nancy, explained that, upon graduating from
high school, he had enlisted in the U.S. Navy. When he left to
start boot camp, he split up with his girlfriend. Upon completing
boot camp, he returned home on leave and his former girlfriend,
Nancy, came to his mother's house where he was staying to talk to
him. She told him that she still loved him, and Bill told her that
he was still in love with her too and wanted to marry her. She then
told him that she was pregnant by another man and that she was
constantly thinking of killing herself. Bill answered that he loved
her with all his heart and that he would marry her right away and
that he would treat the child as his own. Bill told me that he was
so worried about Nancy's mental fragility at that point that he
never returned to the Naval Base.

At the time the divorce was filed, Nancy was already involved
with another man, so she did not mind that Bill had filed for a no

fault divorce. However, she did not want him to get visitation with the son he had raised. She had called the Navy's military police and reported Bill as a "deserter." I also later learned from Bill's military lawyer that Nancy had inquired about a "reward" for turning him in.

Bill was held in the military jail until his court martial about six months later. He pled guilty and I drove to Philadelphia to testify about the circumstances he had related to me that caused him to go AWOL. He was sentenced to time served and an "other than honorable discharge." The custody judge was appalled when I related the back story and awarded Bill visitation rights to his son as if he were actually the biological father. Nancy did seek child support and Bill did not oppose it.

When a client walked into my office for an initial consultation, they either had been served with divorce papers, they thought they wanted to start divorce proceedings, or they knew there were problems in their marriage and just wanted to get an education about the process of divorce and how they would come out. After getting some initial basic information like how long they were married, if there were children of the marriage and how old they were, how each of their incomes compared, and what their assets and debts were, I would then inquire as to the result the client was seeking. My next job was to educate my new client about how the system worked and the claims they could make or be subjected to. Often I would also explain that a lawyer is just a tool needed to get a fair result from the court system and, since lawyers are not trained therapists, in many cases it would be a good idea for the client to hire a counselor or therapist at least for the time they are going through the divorce.

It is very important to remember that a divorce decree is just a piece of paper that makes it possible for you to marry someone else. Very few of my clients were in a big hurry to get remarried, though I did have a few cases in which my client's husband had a pregnant girlfriend and wanted a fast divorce, paying a lot extra for it. Many of my clients did feel that they needed a divorce as quickly as possible in order to move on with their lives though. What is important is that you not become so focused on getting a divorce quickly that you give up rights and assets you are entitled to in order to accomplish that goal. In most states the courts see the marriage as existing from the date of marriage to the date of final separation. Most of the time, intimate relations with others that occur after the final separation are not even considered or held against you. I often advised my clients to let the divorce take the time necessary to get a good result, but that there was no reason not to start dating if they were so inclined. This is a state specific issue, so be sure to discuss it with your attorney.

Appendix C at the end of this book has a section detailing what you should bring with you for the initial consultation with the lawyer.

No Fault Divorce

All 50 states in the USA along with the District of Columbia have *no fault divorce*. A no fault divorce means that the person seeking the divorce does not have to show or prove grounds like adultery or abuse in order to get a divorce. The most common claim made to get a divorce granted is that *irreconcilable differences* exist. The only issue left with respect to getting a divorce is that many states do still require a period of separation from as little as 3 months to as long as two years to get the divorce. With this separation, some states will even allow the party seeking the divorce to show that there has been a separation under the same roof.

Though misconduct no longer needs to be shown to get a divorce, misconduct can still come into play with respect to alimony and custody issues. Even if you have no children and you are not seeking alimony, you should still make your lawyer aware of any misconduct, as the lawyer will often use the misconduct in settlement negations.

What this means is that if one spouse wants a divorce and follows up with having the proper documents filed and served on the other spouse and then waits the required amount of time, there will be a divorce even if the other spouse does not want it. Remember, a divorce decree is just a piece of paper that allows for remarriage. What is far more important is how the assets and debts will be divided and if there will be claims for alimony (spousal support after the divorce) and reimbursement and/or payment of attorney's fees. How these claims are resolved can affect the rest of your life, so this is where you should be focusing your energy.

If claims for property division and/or alimony and/or legal fees are made, the process will be slowed down considerably. In most states, these legal claims must be resolved before a divorce is final, though occasionally in some states the court can do what is called a bifurcated divorce in which the court grants the divorce first and then proceeds to deal with the claims later.

Does It Matter Who Files for Divorce First?

Generally, it does *not* make a difference who files first. In a divorce, the court can be asked in the initial filing or in the possible *answer* filed by the other spouse to divide marital property and debts, to award support, to resolve custody of minor children, and to award legal fees. These claims can be made by the spouse who files first or by the spouse who files second with their answer to the first filing. The only time there may be an advantage to filing first is if there is an urgency to get the courthouse doors open with one of the claims set forth here. As such, if you think your spouse may be hiding marital money or engaging in crazy spending or if your spouse is not giving you money that you need for support or not agreeing about where the children should live, then it may be necessary to file for a divorce ASAP to get the process going to resolve these issues. When it comes to child support or custody however, you can often file legal action outside of a divorce proceeding, since the courts often deal with the issues of custody and child support for people who are not married.

Divorce actions will proceed through three stages:

1. The *pleadings stage* is when the claims are made, either in the initial divorce or in the answer filed by the other person. This is the stage during which you will make claims for property division, custody, support and alimony, and payment of legal fees. This stage will move quickly once you and your lawyer determine what you will need.

2. The *discovery stage* is the stage during which your lawyer will seek to discover what is subject to division and what factors exist that will be beneficial to your case. This will often take the longest period of time. Here, your lawyer will often start by requiring your spouse to answer written questions, to supply documents relating to property, assets, debts, expenses, and tax returns. Often, your lawyer will also have the power to issue subpoenas to financial institutions and employers or anyone else, requiring them to produce documents that may be relevant. Finally, in the discovery stage your lawyer will often have the power to ask your spouse and possibly others to answer questions orally, under oath, before a court reporter. In the discovery stage, your lawyer may need to employ experts like property appraisers and accountants. The discovery stage will end once your lawyer has a complete list (inventory) of the assets, expenses, and debts that are subject to division as well as those that are not and your lawyer should also have a complete list of the specific factors that are relevant to your case like income and educational information, etc. Remember that whatever

your lawyer asks of your spouse will also almost always be asked of you in discovery. Be ready to provide a detailed list of all your expenses, debts, accounts, and assets, along with documents relating to these issues.

During the discovery stage your lawyer should send you copies of everything they obtain. You will get copies of the answers to the written questions your spouse had to answer and copies of all financial documents, appraisals, subpoenas, and the responses, as well as copies of transcripts of the oral depositions that are taken. I would strongly recommend that you read and review everything you get. If you do not understand something, ask your lawyer for an explanation. Remember, a good divorce lawyer has many cases; you have only one. You should be going over everything your spouse turns into the court as you are often the best person to know if something is missing.

3. The *final resolution stage* is the last stage of the divorce. 95% of all divorce cases will end with an agreed settlement contract. 5% will end by going to some form of hearing or trial. The vast majority of divorce cases will end by way of an agreed settlement. This is not because most people are so agreeable but because divorce lawyers know the likely conclusion the court would reach given the circumstance in their case. Most people will listen to their lawyers when they advise them to settle for a result that is in line with what the court would do since moving forward to litigation will not be worth the extra money in the form of legal fees and court costs.

The Collaborative Divorce

A *collaborative divorce* is a process that has grown in popularity in recent time. Although collaborative divorce seems to be a great idea on paper, the sad reality is that, in my experience, it rarely delivers the result it strives for. With a collaborative divorce, the spouses try to agree up front to make full disclosures, put their kids first, and then work with their lawyers and/or mediators to achieve a full and fair settlement amicably without going through the formal processes of the divorce court.

In my experience, even though 90% of divorce cases do end in settlements, collaborative divorces try to achieve the end result often long before both spouses are ready to set aside their anger and emotions to work fairly with each other. A good analogy is that there should never be wars in the world yet, despite the desires of the most brilliant diplomats to avoid war, it still happens. Not only do wars between countries still happen, but they also don't end until one side has been beaten into submission or both sides have agreed that they are losing more than they are gaining.

When emotions and anger are high, the chances that there will be voluntary cooperation are not good. Without voluntary cooperation by spouses who can put aside their anger, fears, and strong emotions, court intervention and the threat of sanctions (punishments) by the judge are needed to move towards a fair result. In too many cases, the collaborative divorce process makes it easier for one spouse to take advantage of the other. In reality, many of the same processes used in collaborative divorce processes are the very same ones used near the end of a divorce case by the mediator or hearing office, but, by the time the spouses are nearing the end of a non-collaborative divorce, they are often more ready to compromise and end their conflict.

7

Property and Debt Division

Inside of a divorce action the court will divide all *marital assets* and *debts*. This division can be a 50/50 equal split or it can be skewed towards one spouse with a different percentage of a split. The court will determine what assets and debts are marital and then it will determine if the split should be something other than equal.

The first thing you need to understand is what assets and debts would be considered marital and subject to division by the courts. For the most part, states have similar laws in this area, but there are some minor differences in some states. Generally, marital assets and debts are those that were acquired between the date of the marriage and the date of the final separation. Often, it will not matter whose name is on a deed or on a car title or on a credit card. If those assets or debts were acquired during the marriage, the court will have jurisdiction and can divide them.

It should also be noted that some assets that one spouse had before the marriage may be divided under certain circumstances. Let's say your spouse had a home in their name before you got married; if during the marriage the mortgage was paid down and/or if that house increased in value because the housing market went up, in many states the increased amount in the value would be considered marital and divided. Pensions, IRAs, and 401 Ks will almost always be in one spouse's name alone, yet the amount that these retirement assets went up in value during the marriage will be considered marital and divided.

The first job for you and your lawyer when it comes to property and debt division is to make a complete list or inventory of these assets and debts. Additionally, you and your lawyer will need to make a list of all assets that are totally non marital like an inheritance, as these separate assets may be a factor that the court will use when deciding what percentage of the marital assets to award to the spouse who has less. These non-marital assets may also be a factor used to determine the length of time that alimony is awarded. Your lawyers' job will be to make a list of all the assets and debts, and in that list your lawyer will need to show if it is marital or nonmarital. The lawyer will also need to show the values at the date of separation and the value today, the date it was acquired, and who has control and possession of the debt or asset now. Additionally, if you or your spouse has what the law calls separate property (like accounts and real estate owned before the marriage or inheritances acquired before or during the marriage) these assets should also be listed with a note as to when and how they were acquired. The more you can do to help with this list like gathering bank statements, etc., the more you will save in legal fees.

Splitting the Assets

"When will the court make a division other than 50/50? Can I get awarded more than half?" There are many factors the divorce court can consider when it comes to how they will make the split of assets and debts and these factors can vary from state to state. The major things the courts will consider in almost all states are:

Difference in incomes and/or earning potential.

Whether your marriage lasted one week or forty years, the differences in the earnings between you and your spouse will be a major factor the divorce courts will use when making decisions with respect to property and debt splits and if post-divorce alimony should be awarded. When one spouse has a much higher income and earning potential, the other spouse is often considered the economically dependent spouse. Because of this, even if there are no children of this marriage and child support is not an issue, it is very important that you provide your lawyer with as much information and documentation you have or can get relating to income. Pay stubs, tax returns, and financial institution statements showing dividend and other income will be needed. Of course, your lawyer can get these, but the more you can provide the more legal fees and time you can save. Future earning potential is also a factor that the courts will often consider. If one spouse has been out of the workforce or if one spouse does the kind of work that could result in an extraordinary increase in income this should be pointed out to the court. Considerations include:

History of educational support.

Most divorce courts will also take it into consideration if one spouse helped the other spouse get or complete an education that increases their earning capacity. If one spouse is working while the other is in school the working spouse may get extra consideration.

Length of the marriage.

The longer the marriage, the more consideration and advantages there are for an economically dependent spouse.

This means that if your spouse has far higher earnings than you do, your chances of getting more than half of the assets and getting a post-divorce alimony award is better.

Minor children and who has custody.

If your spouse has far higher earnings and earning potential and you have full or even 50/50 shared custody, the courts will take this into consideration when determining property division and post-divorce alimony. Divorce courts will often give the majority of the equity in a home to a custodial parent to avoid further disruption of the children's lives.

The total amounts of assets and the total amount of debts.

Here the courts will often use a balancing act. If your spouse earns a lot more than you but there are not a lot of assets to divide, the courts will often give the dependent spouse a bigger share of the assets and longer post-divorce alimony.

Contributions of separate property to the marriage.

Separate property can be property that one spouse had before they got married or that was gifted to them or inherited by them. If the spouse gave the separate property to the marriage or *comingled* the property, this separate property could be transformed into marital property subject to division by the court. This contribution of separate property can be considered by the court in making a division that is not 50/50. Additionally, if one spouse has separate property that they kept separate during the marriage, thus giving that spouse a higher net worth, this factor can also be considered in making the division of marital property. This area of law is discussed in more detail below. It can be different in many states and is an area that should be discussed with your lawyer.

There may be other considerations in some states that the divorce courts will use when it comes to dividing the marital estate. It is a good idea to ask your attorney early on to review with you what factors your state's divorce judges use when it comes to property division.

Marital Property and Debts Versus *Separate* Property and Debts

Generally, all property, assets and debts that were acquired between the marriage and date of final separation will be classified as marital property and the divorce courts will have the authority to divide them. Property, assets and debts that you or your spouse had before you were married or that you inherited can be classified as separate property or *separate debts* in most states.

Separate property can become marital if it is commingled or has increased in value during the marriage. As such, if your spouse owned a home before you were married, it could be considered separate property, but if he added your name to the deed then the courts may decide that he gifted it to the marriage. Additionally, even if your spouse with the home they owned before marriage did not put your name on the deed, a part of that pre-marital home might be subject to division of marital property if that home went up in value because the mortgage was paid down during the marriage or the real estate market in your area went up in value and that separate property home is now worth more than it was when you got married. The same rules can apply to property or assets that you or your spouse inherit during the marriage. If the value goes up because of market forces or the mortgage being paid down, that increase in value alone can be considered the marital portion subject to division.

An example of a portion of separate property becoming marital property with a home is if your spouse's home was worth $100,000.00 on the date you were married and 5 years later when you separate that same home is now worth $150,000.00. Because the mortgage was paid down or the home just went up in value, the increase of $50,000.00 would be considered marital and you would be owed a portion of that increase. The same rule would apply if your spouse had a business or a coin collection; the increase in value during your marriage may be considered marital property to be divided by the divorce court.

Another example might be your spouse's pension or retirement account. Your spouse may have had this account or pension before he married you, but during the marriage it went up in value because of interest and/or additional money contributions. That increase in value would be something the divorce court would divide.

Debts or money owed can also be classified into marital and non-marital categories. If your spouse had a credit card in his name alone before he married you but then your spouse charged more items to that card during your marriage, the increase in debt could be considered a marital debt for which both of you are responsible.

What Is Considered Separate Property that the Courts Cannot Split?

What is considered separate property and what portion can be considered marital can vary from state to state so please be sure to discuss this with your attorney. In most states property that one spouse had before the marriage or property that was gifted to them or inherited may be considered separate property that will remain that spouse's after a divorce and is not subject to division in a divorce. In many states however, separate property can be converted to marital property by the spouse that owns it by commingling it with marital property (example: adding money earned during the marriage to an account that was held prior to marriage) or by adding a spouse's name to the deed. Additionally, in most states the appreciation of separate property during the marriage will be considered marital (example: husband's coin collection worth $10,000.00 on the date of marriage but at the date of separation it is worth $50,000.00, because the value went up during the marriage. The $40,000.00 increase in value of the coin collection *might* be considered a marital asset in many states. Some states do differentiate between passive increases like if the collection only went up because the market went up over time and not because of anything the spouse/owner did and active appreciation like if the husband added new coins to the collection during the marriage.)

When it comes to debts that either party had prior to marriage, here again, many states have different rules and the debt, if it still exists on the date of final separation, might be considered separate or marital depending on the circumstances.

It is important that you tell your lawyer about every asset and debt both you and your spouse have, including those that you had prior to getting married or that were gifted to either of you or inherited. Your lawyer will need to know when the asset or debt was acquired, what it was worth at different time periods and how it was used and held during the marriage.

Typical Assets and How the Courts May Deal with Them

Marital Home.

When it comes to the home you and your spouse acquired

during your marriage, the court has only three options: award it to you, award it to your spouse, or order it sold and if there is any money realized from the sale, divide it. If you want the marital home, the court will consider who remained in the home after separation; do you have custody of minor children who would benefit by staying in the home; can you afford to service the debt on the home with your income and any child support and/or alimony you may have or be getting. If there is a lot of equity in the home (home value less all home debt/mortgages = equity) the court will determine if there are other marital assets that can be awarded to your spouse to offset their share of the equity that they would have gotten.

In most states the divorce court does have the power to give one spouse exclusive possession of the marital home while the divorce is going forward. The divorce court may also have the power in many states to order the spouse who is not in the home to pay all or part of the mortgage as part of their child or spousal support obligation.

The courts also have the power to give one spouse the home yet require the other spouse to stay on the mortgage or to allow one spouse to stay in the marital home for a certain period of time (which can be years) to keep the kids in their normal environment and then, at a later time order the house sold and the profits split.

You and your husband may reach an agreement that one of you will get the ownership of the marital home. It is important to remember that although it is easy for one of you to sign a new deed giving the other the ownership, if there is a mortgage you often cannot easily get a person's name off that mortgage. The deed shows who owns the house but the mortgage shows who has a legal obligation to pay the debt. The mortgage holder (often a bank), must approve removing the name of a debtor and most of the time the bank will not give this approval as it is in their best interest to keep as many names on the debt as possible. In order to remove a name the house/property will usually need to be refinanced or a new loan taken out paying off the old mortgage. This can often be a problem as many times one spouse alone will not qualify for a new mortgage.

With respect to getting a name removed from a mortgage, the solution commonly used in property settlements is to give the spouse receiving the home a set period of time/ years to refinance or sell the property. It is also common to require the spouse receiving the home to show evidence that they have at least applied on a yearly or biyearly basis to refinance the home. Finally, it is not uncommon for the spouse who is staying on the mortgage to insist on a clause in the final settlement that would state that if the spouse who is required to pay the mortgage becomes delinquent (falls behind on the payments) that the house can be ordered sold immediately so that the non-owning spouse's credit is not affected.

Pensions, IRAs, 401 Ks.

Although pensions, IRAs and 401 Ks are always in only one spouse's name, the amounts put into these retirement type assets during the marriage will be considered marital. Additionally, the increase in value of these types of assets during the marriage will also be considered marital and subject to division in the divorce. The most common way to make a division used by the courts is to order a transfer of some of the funds into the other spouse's name by moving these funds into a retirement fund for them. With pensions your lawyer will often need to hire an expert to determine the value of the marital portion. Many times, instead of moving the money in these retirement funds the court may use the amount one spouse is entitled to as an offset against another asset like giving one spouse the entire pension and the other spouse all the equity in the marital home.

The funds in most retirement type accounts are often pre-tax (this means no income taxes have been paid on this money). It is important to know that there is a procedure where retirement funds can be split without incurring any tax consequences or penalties. This is done by moving the funds from one spouse's account to the other but keeping the funds in a retirement type account like an IRA. Often to avoid taxes when these retirement funds are being divided the attorney will have a judge sign a QDRO (Qualified Domestic Relations Order).

Financial accounts.

With respect to financial accounts like savings accounts, stock brokerage and mutual funds, etc., the divorce courts will often use the value at the time of separation before making the divisions. It is important to note here that in most states the divorce courts have the power to issue a freeze order to stop the dissipation by one spouse of money in these accounts. Your lawyer will have this freeze order served on the financial institution so that the money does not disappear. The divorce court can also order some of the funds released to a spouse who needs them before the divorce is final.

As stated previously, it is not uncommon for one spouse to begin anticipating a divorce long before the other. That spouse may be channeling money out to hidden accounts or into other people's/relatives' names to hold for them. It is critical that your lawyer go back three to five years when seeking financial statements and it is important that the documents that are obtained be reviewed at least by you and possibly by a forensic accountant to see if there are any funds that left these accounts without a good explanation.

Automobiles.

When it comes to automobiles, here again, these assets which were acquired during the marriage are marital property regardless of in whose name they are titled. Their net value (book value at time of separation minus the amount owed equals net value) is subject to division in the divorce so, if one spouse's car is worth more than the other spouse's car, the courts will make an offset.

Furniture, collections, jewelry, and other personal property.

All furniture, jewelry, stamp, coin, and other collections acquired during the marriage are considered marital property subject to division in the divorce. The market value (value it will sell for) is often the value on the date of separation. Your lawyer will need a list of these types of assets along with an indication of which spouse has possession and who wants it. You will often just guess at the market value and if there is a dispute regarding who will get which items, your lawyer can get an expert to appraise them.

Businesses.

If you or your spouse owns a business that was started or purchased during the marriage this business will be considered a marital asset subject to division in the divorce. With businesses, your lawyer will probably need an expert to determine the valuation. Many times businesses will be classified as being personal or non-personal in nature and this can affect the value.

Even if the business was owned by your spouse prior to marriage, in many states the increased value during the marriage will be subject to division by the court. This area is one to discuss with your attorney if you or your spouse have a business or own any part of a business, even if it is in a corporate name or is a LLC (Limited Liability Corporation).

Gifts.

Many states will divide gifts into two categories: gifts to the marriage and separate non-marital property. In most states, gifts from one spouse to the other will be considered marital property, subject to division and included in the marital pot. Generally, gifts to both of you like wedding gifts will also be considered marital property regardless of which side of the family they came from. In some states even the engagement ring is considered marital property even though it was gifted before the marriage. When it comes to gifts, I would recommend you discuss this with your attorney as the laws vary from state to state.

Finding Hidden Assets

It is not unusual for one spouse to know way ahead of the other that the marriage will eventually be headed to divorce court. If that spouse that has foreknowledge of the impending divorce is also the one who makes the most money, it is not uncommon for that spouse to try to hide funds and assets that normally would be divided in the divorce. If you think that your spouse might have hidden money or assets so that you do not get a share of them, it is critical before hiring one of the lawyers you interview to ask what actions they can and will take to try to find these assets.

Your lawyer's first job will be to ask your spouse questions in writing (interrogatories), request documents regarding financial assets from your spouse and financial institutions, and possibly ask questions in person (deposition) that must be answered truthfully under penalty of perjury or under oath. Your lawyer should be going backwards three to five years with these requests for information. Your first job will be to gather any documents you can find from any financial institutions and to provide your lawyer with the names of financial institutions in which your spouse might have an account.

You and your lawyer should be reviewing the answers to the *discovery* your spouse has provided, looking for unexplained withdrawals of larger than ordinary amounts of money. Your lawyer may want to hire a forensic accountant to further review the documents. Your attorney can also issue subpoenas to banks and financial institutions, looking for statements in your spouse's name and in the name of any corporations, partnerships, and LLCs in which your spouse may have an interest. Additionally, you and your lawyer should be adding up all deposits your spouse has made in each year and comparing that total to the total income your spouse has claimed on his tax return. Discrepancies should be an additional area of inquiry.

Finally, your lawyer should structure any settlement to include a provision stating that if it is later discovered your spouse did not make full disclosure of financial assets, this will be grounds to reopen the divorce to seek a share of the non-disclosed assets plus a penalty and legal fees.

8

Post-Divorce Alimony

Almost all states have alimony, which is support for a spouse after the divorce. How long and under what circumstances alimony will be awarded is state specific. Some states tend to be better for men and other states are considered better for women. One of the important questions to ask lawyers in your initial interview is how your state views alimony, what factors are considered for alimony, and how long the alimony award can last.

Length of the marriage and the disparity (difference) in incomes and earning potential are often the biggest factors when it comes to an alimony award. In most states, alimony will end if the person receiving it gets remarried, and in some states, alimony can end if the receiving spouse starts living with a person of the opposite sex under certain circumstances. The amount of assets/property/money awarded to the alimony seeking spouse can also often be a factor. If there is a big earning difference but not much money is awarded in the divorce, the alimony can be greater or for a longer period. The opposite can also be true. If the receiving spouse has custody of minor children, this can also be a determining factor.

Since most divorces end with an agreed upon settlement, it may also be possible to negotiate away alimony ending factors like remarriage or cohabitation. I have negotiated alimony awards where the receiving woman has remarried and is still getting alimony from her former spouse.

Another key point with alimony is the circumstances under which it is *modifiable* (can be increased or decreased). If the payer's income goes up, can a request be made to increase the alimony? If the payer's income goes down or the receiver's income goes up, can the alimony go down? Generally, in most states, if the court orders alimony after a full trial, that alimony is modifiable/changeable if a change in circumstances occurs. At the same time, it is common for alimony to be listed as non-modifiable in settlement agreements, since often the receiver wants the assurance that this income stream will remain and the payer wants the assurance that they will not be hit for more if their pay goes up.

Often the starting point for alimony will be based on the amount of money the spouse has already been awarded as spousal support or pre-divorce alimony. From there, the courts will often closely look at the future possible earning potential of each person. Even in a short marriage, if one spouse can show they are going to school trying to increase their earning potential, the courts are often more likely to make an alimony award for a fixed period of time so that the spouse can complete that education. In long term marriages, the courts will often focus on the standard of living the couple had when they were together and look to do as much as possible to try to help the dependent spouse maintain that standard of living. Lifetime alimony also exists under some circumstances, like long marriages, in many states.

Finally, it is important to look at how much money each spouse will receive from Social Security upon retirement. Some courts will divide the difference in Social Security as marital property while others will take a big difference into consideration in an alimony award.

My strongest recommendation when it comes to alimony is to get several opinions from lawyers in your state and county as to what your chances are of getting it and how long that award can be for in your situation. Judges in each state try to be consistent so there is no reason an experienced divorce attorney cannot give you an educated opinion as to your likely result. If you cannot get an opinion as to your chances for alimony, the amount you are likely to get, and for how long, look for a different lawyer, and, if the opinions are not all similar, rule out the lawyer that comes in far apart from the others. It is also a good idea to discuss with your lawyer the actions that can end your alimony or prevent you from getting it. As stated previously, depending on your state, living with someone of the opposite sex may hamper or prevent an alimony award.

Once you have a good idea as to whether you are likely to be awarded alimony and for how long, then you should start thinking about what additional terms and conditions you would like to have your lawyer negotiate for, including what circumstances would end your alimony early and whether you would want it modifiable should your or your spouse's circumstances change. A discussion with a CPA is always a good idea when it comes to alimony.

9

Attorney's Fees

Getting Your Spouse to Pay Your Legal Fees, Court Costs, and Expert Fees

In addition to asking the divorce court to divide your property and debts, determine custody, and order support, you can ask the court to order your spouse to pay your legal fees in the divorce, if your spouse earns significantly more money than you do. Like alimony, every state is different, and some are better than others when it comes to ordering the payment of legal fees.

It is important to know that even if your spouse can be ordered to pay your legal fees, often this will be in the form of reimbursing you for amounts you have already paid and/or paying a balance that is owed to your lawyer. Almost all lawyers will require that you pay them what is called a *retainer* in order for them to start representing you. One of the things to be sure to ask at the initial consultation of the lawyer is how much of a retainer the lawyer requires to begin to represent you. Lawyers generally sell their time by charging an hourly rate and this amount will be charged against the initial retainer that you will likely pay when hiring the lawyer. In some states, the lawyer does not need to wait until the end of the case to get the spouse who earns more to pay some of their legal fees. A court order for payment of legal fees before the end of the case is often called an *interim legal fee order*. In addition to legal fees, in many states your lawyer can ask the court to have your spouse pay for experts they must hire like appraisers, psychologists, and accountants as well as for court costs.

As you may have already figured out, legal fees and other divorce costs can get expensive. Ideally, an aggressive lawyer will do everything possible to shift a lot of those fees and costs onto your spouse, but, at the initial consultation, you should ask the lawyer what actions they will take against your higher earning spouse, when those actions will be taken, and if, after the initial retainer you pay runs out, they will try to get your spouse to pay before looking to you for payment. Your lawyer should also be able to give you a well-educated opinion as to the likelihood of getting your spouse to pay some or all of your legal fees and costs.

Many times clients of mine would have to borrow money from relatives and friends to pay an initial retainer and if this happens, be sure to let your lawyer know the source of all money you pay them so that they can let the court know when they make a claim for legal fees on your behalf. Of course, if you know your marriage may be heading to divorce court, you should be doing everything possible to stockpile and save money to cover legal fees and expenses. I have also had many cases where I obtained a *freeze order* on all assets and bank accounts and then went back to the court to ask the judge to unfreeze some funds so that the costs and fees could be paid.

In addition to the earnings of each spouse, another factor that the divorce courts will often look at when it comes to ordering legal fees is what assets the economically dependent, lower earning spouse is likely to be awarded in the divorce. If the court believes that by the end of the case the lower earning spouse will have more than enough to cover the legal fees by selling some assets, then the court might not order the legal fees paid by the other spouse. If you feel you might fall into this category, it is important to ask your lawyer at the outset if they will allow you to run up a legal fee debt with them until the end when you will get enough to pay them.

Another factor that a divorce court may take into consideration is whether the higher earning spouse (or the spouse with the most money available from any source) is using money as a weapon by having their lawyer file lots of legal proceedings for the sole purpose of costing their spouse more money so that they may have to surrender or take a less than adequate settlement. This tactic is not uncommon and protracting the litigation to run up fees can also happen if your spouse's lawyer is less than ethical and runs up fees primarily because they know their client can afford them. A diligent divorce lawyer can make a claim on your behalf for legal fees even when your spouse and you earn about the same money if they can show that the other side is protracting the litigation to run up the fees and costs. Often your lawyer can show the court correspondence where they offered to voluntarily provide documentation, yet the other side still filed a formal motion. Other tactics used to run up legal fees and costs are: constantly filing motions with respect to trivial matters; not complying with court orders; requiring additional correspondence and motions; failing to provide documents or answer discovery in the time period required, thus requiring additional motions to compel; and failing to show up for scheduled hearings.

Another factor in awarding legal fees that the courts will consider even with spouses who have the same earnings is whether one spouse has funds from an outside source available and the other does not.

The bottom line when it comes to legal fees is that most divorce courts do strive to "level the playing field," and awards of legal fees and costs are often needed to make this happen. Unfortunately, some states are less inclined than others to make this happen, but, regardless of which state you are in, the claim for legal fees should be made if your spouse has more funds available than you do or if your spouse seems to be making the case more expensive than it needs to be.

10

Negotiating Settlements

At the initial consultation, I would tell my clients, "You have two choices: you can use your money to pay for your children's college education or you can use your money to pay for my children's college education. It all comes down to how much you and your spouse can settle among yourselves."

You have two choices: you can use your money to pay for your children's college education or you can use your money to pay for my children's college education.

For you to properly negotiate and not cheat yourself, it is critical that you have a good idea of the likely result if your case goes forward to a judge. This way, you are not negotiating against yourself. If you know what the likely result will be with a judge, you can make an informed decision and hopefully end up with about the same result. With this critical knowledge, you will know when to walk away from the table and refuse to take an offer that is far less than you would get by going to court. You can also tell your spouse that it is silly to give lawyers a bunch of money to get a result that you can both reach yourselves. Even if your spouse does not initially believe you when you inform him about what your lawyer told you, your spouse will often go back to his lawyer to verify the information and then come back to the table to talk.

In about 60% of my cases both spouses were able to reach a settlement on at least part of their issues. I would tell clients that even if they cannot settle all their issues in their divorces, they should be able to at least reach an agreement on some of them. 75% of my clients with children reached an agreement with respect to custody and visitation. About 30% were able to resolve their entire divorce early on before they had to spend a lot of money on legal fees. My advice was that when they could reach agreements on anything, they should write it up themselves, sign and date the agreement, and turn it in to their lawyer who could convert it to a fully legal settlement.

With respect to all claims that can be made in a divorce, be they a request for support, custody, property/debt division, or legal fees, the divorce courts are set up to require that you attempt to negotiate a settlement before a judge hears your case. It is also common for the lawyers to send settlement offers to each other before moving forward to any litigation.

90% of my cases did end with a settlement at some point. Many times those settlements did not come about until the lawyers had completed all discovery, like requiring written answers to pages and pages of written questions, requiring each side to produce reams of financial documents, questioning the other spouse under oath with a court reporter, and hiring experts to examine what they obtained. Most of the time, you and your spouse will end up in a room with your lawyer and a mediator, hearing officer, or judge, who is going to tell you that the settlement offer now differs very little from what a judge will eventually decide and that, if you settle now, you can potentially resolve this issue or all your issues without the added time or expense.

Often, because one spouse is not voluntarily forthcoming

and honestly providing all the information that is needed to make a proper property division, the attorneys have no choice but to follow all the formal methods of information gathering. If the attorney skips steps, they can be responsible for their client not getting all they are entitled to. If your spouse lies or hides info after formal discovery, the case can often be reopened later. However, if your assets are not complex and you do not believe that there is anything you do not know about, the only things that would prevent a reasonable settlement are ego and anger.

Many times, my goal when I was cross examining the opposing spouse was to try and make them as angry as possible. I did this because I knew that when a person is experiencing strong emotions, they do not have good self-control, and I was more likely to get testimony that would hurt them and their case. My goal with my own clients was to do everything possible to keep them from letting strong emotions cloud their thinking. I would tell my clients that almost no one knows them as well as their spouse and that their spouse knows exactly which buttons to push to get them angry and emotional and to lose self-control.

Realities and Recommendations When Considering a Settlement

Reality. Most settlements will end the issue or even your entire case.
It is difficult and often impossible once you have an agreement to come back and change it. There will always be a huge temptation to "get it over with" and move on with your life, but you never want to be in a position of regret that you should have had a better result once the stress of the case has worn off. When you do settle, you want to feel that you got what you were entitled to, that you got close to or better than

what you would have ended up with from a judge.

Recommendation.

Be aware of the range you should get from a judge and go into the settlement conference or mediation with your batteries fully charged. Consider taking a short vacation first so you can do some deep thinking and leave your life's issues behind. When you come back, you will be in a better position to stand firm when you need to and not buckle under just to get it over with. Decide in advance what is most important to you and stand firm on those issues, but compromise on the issues that are not as important.

Reality. Divorces and all the issues and claims that go along with them can be emotionally devastating.

If you want to reach a reasonable and fair settlement so you can move forward with your life sooner and save money in legal fees, you will need to do your best to get beyond your anger and fear so that you can think logically. You don't want your anger to prevent you from accepting a fair settlement; You don't want your anger to cause you to take the case to a full trial when you will only end up with the same or even a worse result. On the other hand, you don't want your fear to control you so that you accept an unfair settlement simply to end the process sooner.

Recommendation.

It's always a good idea when possible to find a good therapist to regularly talk to while you are going through your divorce. Understanding and working through the issues, emotions and hot buttons can do wonders to prepare you so that you can have full control of your own mental faculties when you walk into a settlement conference or mediation.

Reality. Mediators and others who are charged with "helping" facilitate the settlement are not necessarily fair or impartial.

Often, these mediators are judged themselves by how many cases they are able to settle and not how fair the results were. Because of this, some mediators will focus on the spouse that they perceive to be more likely to compromise and push that person into accepting a settlement that is less than they should have gotten. This is why it is so important that you have a good understanding of the likely result if the case were to go to a judge. That way, even if you take a little less to avoid the expense and time in going to trial, you are at least making an informed decision.

Recommendation.

Pad your requests up at the start. If you want $30.00 ask for $50.00. This way you can appear to be compromising even when you end up with what you really want. Don't be afraid to stand firm on your important issues and never be afraid to temporarily walk away from the table. When you are standing firm on an important issue point out all the issues that you have or are willing to compromise on. Portray yourself as the reasonable spouse who is mostly compromising to end things but that on this important issue it's not fair to have you take less.

Reality. There are some lawyers who dislike going to trial.

Some lawyers really dislike going to trial, and these lawyers may be tempted to push their clients into accepting a settlement that is far less than they would have gotten by going to a full hearing before a judge. Other times, a lawyer may push their client into a far less than ideal settlement, because they want to be paid their outstanding legal fees sooner rather than later. Once your case is over, the lawyer will just move on to their next case, but you will be forever stuck with the settlement that was made. The bottom line is that you are the one responsible for yourself, and you should never let yourself be pushed into any settlement that you are not comfortable with.

Recommendation.

When you are interviewing lawyers, find out how often they have actually gone to full trials. Make sure your lawyer understands in advance what is important to you and what your bottom line is. Also make it clear that you would rather go to trial and that you have no problem holding out for what you want. If you are being pushed to move off a position that is important to you, stand firm. Don't get so focused on one tree (getting a settlement) that you lose sight of the forest (what you should be getting). Too many times lawyers and their clients make the primary goal reaching any settlement rather than reaching a fair settlement.

Reality. For a settlement to be fair, both spouses must be on a level playing field.

As stated previously, at least 90% of all cases will end with a settlement, but for a settlement to be fair, both spouses must be on a level playing field at the outset. Many experts agree that, if you have been a victim of physical or mental abuse, you will probably not be starting out on a level field, as your spouse has established a pattern of assuming power over you and manipulating you into accepting this imbalance of power. If you have been the victim of mental or physical abuse, it may actually be better to go into the settlement or mediation with a clear and fair bottom line on every issue and insist on just going to trial rather than trying to compromise below this pre-established floor.

Recommendation.
If you have been a victim of physical or mental abuse during your marriage, it is not just important for you to have a personal therapist as soon as possible after your separation; it is critical. No one should ever be conditioned to accept abuse as justified, deserved, or normal and there is a high likelihood that your mentally or physically abusive spouse did this to you. Your spouse slowly and methodically chipped away at your self-esteem and self-worth. Unless you have worked with a good therapist to reverse the damage that the abuse has done to your sense of self, it is impossible to end up with a fair settlement. It is more likely if you do settle that over time you will regret your agreement when you realize that others with similar financial circumstances did far better than you. Bottom line is that, if you fear your spouse, I would not advise you to settle in mediation or, if possible, I would suggest that you not even go to a settlement conference or mediation. You are never on a level playing field if you are afraid of the other spouse. Yes, a full trial will be more expensive and take longer than a settlement, but, for abuse victims, a full trial will most often end in a better result.

This is an area where many lawyers do not have enough experience to be proper advocates. Additionally, many lawyers may not be fully aware of the level of abuse their clients may have been subjected to by their spouse, because their clients may not have fully shared all the details of their experiences due to embarrassment or shame. If you have been a victim of mental or physical abuse, it is important that your lawyer know as much as possible about what you have experienced.

Reality. Judges are just humans and, as in any profession, there are some who are far better than others.
Judges, like most of us, make mistakes and can have or develop prejudices against one spouse. Often the judge is not fair, and there are times when judges make terrible mistakes with their

decisions. You will always have the right to appeal a judge's decision, but the person who appeals will be in an uphill battle with the odds stacked against them. The fact that judges make mistakes and that there are no guarantees that the judge will be fair makes it even more important to try to be reasonable and reach a settlement even if you do not get everything you wanted as long as you can live with the result. You need a lawyer you can fully trust to guide you in the settlement process.

Recommendation.

Discuss appeals with your lawyer even before your trial. Do your best to get all information that makes you more sympathetic to the judge out there and on the record. Sometimes in divorce, like in everything else, life is not fair. Often, your only choice is to just accept the result and do your best to move on with your life.

11

Coming Out Ahead in Your Divorce

An old adage among businessmen is "Slow to hire, fast to fire." When picking a lawyer for your divorce you are making a decision that could affect the rest of your life. You will often feel that you need to act quickly, but it is critically important that you take the time and do the legwork to choose the right attorney for you. Picking a lawyer is the first chapter of this book for a reason. You need to be able to fully trust your lawyer and know that he or she is fully competent and has your best interests as a priority. Your divorce lawyer must be fully versed in the law in your state *and* be able and willing to communicate effectively with you so that you understand at all times what is going on with your case and what the specific goals are each step of the way.

The "fast to fire" rule also applies. It will cost you to replace your lawyer with a new one; you will be paying twice to educate a new lawyer, since the new attorney will need to spend time getting fully acquainted with your case. That being said, if you do not fully trust that your attorney is as versed in divorce law as they should be or is just not being fully effective (or seems to be outgunned and losing a lot to your spouse's attorney), it can often be a mistake not to switch lawyers. There is no reason you cannot set up consultation appointments with new lawyers while still being represented by your current attorney.

It is also important that you have realistic goals and expectations. Many times, in my divorce practice one of my first jobs was to bring my client "back down to earth". This means that when my potential client first walked into my office, the results they were seeking were just not possible given the circumstances and the law. I was always blunt, honest, and candid right up front when telling them that the results they were seeking were just not going to happen. Of course, I then followed up with the likely results in their case. If the client continued to insist and hold on to their unrealistic expectations, I would not take the case since it did my reputation no good to have an unhappy client at the end. Unfortunately, there are attorneys who are desperate enough for the retainer that they don't deal with a client's unrealistic expectations honestly. As stated earlier, there were many times when I suggested to clients that it seemed only castration would satisfy them and that this option was not available to me given the current state of the law.

In reality, most of my clients actually had lower expectations than the likely results in their cases, and often the clients were thrilled to hear my predictions as to how their cases would probably end. For many clients, having the financial ability to retain an attorney and support their household until the courts could enter orders for support was a problem. This is why having a financial war chest or rainy-day fund saved up is so important. If you think this will be an issue for you, be sure to communicate this potential problem with your attorney at the outset. In most states, emergency motions and remedies are available to experienced lawyers. Do not let embarrassment keep you from communicating fully with your attorney on any issue ever.

Initial Preparation

Once you feel that there are serious problems with your marriage, the first thing that you need to do is get an education. At many of my initial consultations, the clients were not really ready to move forward with a divorce. Instead, they were meeting with me to get educated about how they would end up if a divorce happened. It is important for you to know as quickly as possible how a divorce will affect you in your state; what steps and procedures are likely in your case; what you should or shouldn't do with respect to your marital home and who should move out; and where you will stand when it comes to money and financial considerations.

When trying to get an education on divorce, custody, and support, not all lawyers are good teachers, so it is important that you visit several attorneys and ask them all the same questions. Yes, you will possibly spend a little more paying for several initial consultations, but, in life, all education comes at some cost. Besides getting a better education by visiting several lawyers, you will also be in a better position to feel out which lawyer will be the best fit for you. It is also a lot less expensive to see several lawyers up front than to change lawyers midstream.

Another benefit of a good education in this area is that you will learn what documents you need to start collecting and what documents you need to start preparing. You should walk out of the lawyer's office with a list of documents you can try to obtain like tax returns, bank statements, etc. You should also know what kind of documents you can start preparing, like inventories and lists of assets and debts, as well as lists detailing problems with your spouse as they might relate to custody.

Separation

Once you or your spouse or both of you have made the decision not to continue to live together, a decision may have to be made about who will move out. If your spouse moves out, obviously no further decision on this issue needs to be made. But if you want a separation and your spouse is not moving out, there needs to be a discussion with your lawyer.

Generally, if there are children and you want to have primary custody, staying in the home and having your spouse move out will be to your advantage. As stated in the custody chapter, judges will usually not want to disrupt the children's routines, so being in possession of the marital residence will give you an edge. Do not assume that you should leave just because your spouse can better afford to pay the home's expenses. Your lawyer can discuss support options so that the financial obligations are not an issue. If your spouse is insisting on staying in the marital residence, then you should discuss the methods available to the court to force them to move. Another possible option when a spouse won't move is to find a residence that will accommodate the children in the same school district and take the kids with you when you do move.

If there are neither children nor custody issues to consider, then you will still want to discuss with your attorney the possible downside of moving out yourself. In some states, moving out of the marital residence can be considered abandonment and could make you the person at fault, thus impacting your ability to get financial support in some instances. Additionally, if you move out, you may still have obligations towards the debt of a jointly owned home. A lawyer who is a competent divorce specialist should be able to guide you with respect to this issue.

Ongoing Preparation

Once you have an attorney you trust, there are a few things you can do to help your attorney be as effective as possible. First, when you talk to your lawyer, in person or by phone, take notes. I had many clients even bring in small portable recorders and ask permission to record our conversations. This can now even be done with most phones. I never minded being recorded. You should still write up summaries of the conversations with careful attention to the stated goals. Remember, lawyers sell their time and you do not want to be wasting that time going over the same information over and over. You also don't want to be using your lawyer as a therapist. Lawyers are more expensive than therapists and are not trained to be effective in that role. You want your lawyer to have the information they can use to help your case, but when it comes to your emotional needs, a good therapist can do more for you.

A good lawyer will schedule time to meet and prepare you for every hearing you will attend. You should understand fully why the hearing is being held and what your lawyer's objectives and goals are. You should also know what you should be saying when it is your turn to talk so that you are maximally effective. If you have a written list of subjects that you need to cover, organized as bullet points listed in order of importance, this can be a big help. You and your lawyer should each have a copy of these bullet points, and you should review your answers with your lawyer, paying close attention to the attorney's advice. You will also discuss your spouse's expected testimony along with your possible answers to your spouse's claims. Ideally, there should be no surprises for your lawyer and your job is to help your attorney anticipate what your spouse will say.

If you really want to come out ahead in your divorce, you need to stay informed, understand what is going on, and be aware of what the goal is each step of the way. Just like a restaurant will have only one chef, your job is not to take over your lawyer's job and tell the chef what recipes to use; instead, your job is to provide the food that the chef will use in the recipes. This means that before you even receive any mailed documents from your lawyer, you know they are coming and what they are. By understanding what is going on in your case and what the goal is with each step, you can focus on providing all the information you have that is relevant to that goal. Yes, at the outset you filled up the lawyer's/chef's pantry with "food," but your lawyer has many cases and you have just one. If you fully understand what the lawyer wants to accomplish at each step, you can "remind" your lawyer of the points that best fit the goals/recipes. You never want to be in a position of leaving a hearing wondering why an important piece of information was not communicated to the judge.

The bottom line is that the better prepared you and your lawyer are for whatever is happening in your case, the better chance you have of being satisfied with the result. By picking a lawyer with whom you are comfortable communicating and who you feel will be able and willing to communicate with you, the better your chances are that you will come out with a fair result and really be ahead where it counts.

Know When to Settle and Know When to Just Say "No"

The divorce courts are set up to push and encourage settlements in every area (custody, property division, and support). The courts could never handle the volume and amount of work if a judge had to make all the decisions. Additionally, the judges feel that if people reach decisions and settlements among themselves, they are more likely to abide by those agreements, and the courts will not be called upon as often to provide enforcement. The reality is that 90% of the issues will be resolved and ended because of a settlement. The unfortunate reality is that too many times a spouse settles for less than what is fair and less than what they would have gotten by refusing to settle and going to a judge for a decision.

You've got to know when to hold 'em, know when to fold 'em,
Know when to walk away, know when to run.
(Lyrics from The Gambler by Kenny Rogers)

The key to coming out ahead is that when you do reach a settlement, the resolution should be one that is fair and you should not end up with less than you would have probably gotten had you insisted on letting a judge make the decision. In order for this to happen there are two critical factors: first, you should know before you walk into a settlement room (or discuss the issue with your spouse if you will try to settle yourself) what the likely result would be if the matter went to a judge to decide. Of course, no lawyer can give you an absolute guaranteed result, but a good, highly experienced divorce attorney can give you a good opinion about the most probable result. Yes, there is always a chance that the lawyer's opinion could be wrong, and the judge could give you far less, but, with an experienced attorney, the probability of that happening should be low.

The second key factor in getting a fair settlement and coming out ahead is knowing when to compromise and when to hold firm. This factor is totally up to you. If you know the likely probable result from a judge, then, when it comes time to settle, you can decide if it's worth it to you to hold firm for at least that result or better or to take a little less to get a speedy, less costly result. Even if you take less, at least you will know that it was your decision and be able to better live with it. Just remember, that even though the divorce battle may seem terrible while it's happening, a year after it is all over you do not want to regret that you did not get all that you were probably entitled to.

Coming Out Ahead When in Front of a Judge

Before you are ever in court you should know the specific issues on which the judge's decision will be based. Your lawyer should provide you with his bullet points of the areas of testimony he will be covering with you. The bullet points should be specific enough that you can figure out what the questions will be so that you can formulate your answers in your head. You do not want to write out your answers and try to memorize them. Doing this will often cause you to be less believable than you could be. Instead, you want to focus on the facts and information you will want to talk about when you are asked questions. Going over the bullet points ahead of time with your attorney and discussing the information and facts you will talk about in response to his questions will also give your attorney a good opportunity to refresh his memory about your case. It will also give the attorney a chance to make suggestions to improve your answers and to make sure you cover the most important facts thoroughly.

At this pre-hearing meeting with your attorney, you should also be discussing the possible points and issues your spouse will raise and the responses that you should make to them. Many times, if there is something that you know your spouse will be bringing out that may hurt your case, it is often a good idea to bring it up first if possible. This way your counter response can come in early and the sting can be minimized.

In my experience the most common reason for a negative result from a judge is the losing attorney's failure to properly prepare. Properly preparing means that not only is the lawyer ready to argue and present his case but that the client has also been properly prepared so that both the client and the attorney know what will be presented to the judge. The bullet points listing the information that will be presented should be prioritized with the facts that will help support your case most, then going down in order of importance. Ideally, you should be prepared with enough knowledge of the points you will need to make that your nervousness is lessened because you always know what is coming and how you will answer.

When your spouse is testifying, be ready to take notes listing the points they have made that you want to rebut or refute. This way, before it is your lawyer's turn to question your spouse (cross examine), you and your attorney can review what your spouse said that you do not agree with, what your spouse said that is not true, and what your spouse said that you feel requires an explanation or additional facts that your lawyer can try to bring out with your spouse or with you when you are back on the stand.

Remember that it is your lawyer's job to determine what is most important to bring out to the judge both in your testimony and in his cross examination of your spouse. Just because your spouse lied about something does not mean your lawyer has to refute it. Your lawyer knows that the judge's attention span has limits and your lawyer will want to spend the most time on the issues and facts that are most likely to help you get the result you want. Not every lie needs to be corrected and not every fact you know needs to be in the record. Your lawyer will need to have the final say as to how your case should be presented. Remember, only one chef in the kitchen; you provide the food, but the lawyer decides how it will be prepared. An experienced domestic law attorney will have probably been before the same judge on other cases and will also know what biases that judge seems to have. You will need to listen to your attorney and let them make the strategic decisions.

Regardless of how the case comes out and what the judge decides, you want to know that you did all that was possible to get that judge to fully understand your position and the rationale for your getting the result you want. You also want the judge to believe what you tell them and the best way to accomplish this is to give your version of the facts in a clear and natural manner. The key word here is "natural." It is not natural not to be angry or upset when describing something you think is terrible so just let your normal emotions be there. You can ask for a break anytime you want to compose yourself. Picture yourself just telling a friend what happened and try to testify in the same manner. When your spouse's attorney has their turn to question you (cross examine) that attorney will do their best to confuse you, to rattle you, and to make you say things that you don't mean to say. The best advice I would have is to take some control back by slowing things down. When you are asked a question, pause long enough to repeat the question to yourself and think about your answer before giving it. Never get into an argument with your spouse's lawyer. That is not your job. Just do your best to remain calm no matter how much you are provoked. Never forget what you are seeking and why you are seeking it.

12

Moving on After Divorce

(Chapter contributed by Dr. Elizabeth Jenkins)

The divorce is done. You expected to feel ecstatic. Instead, you may feel battle weary. Perhaps you feel relief as well as sadness. You may even be unsure exactly what it is that you are feeling. Even good losses are losses. Think about it. You've spent a great deal of time, possibly even years, to get to this point, to be free from your ex. You've eaten, slept, and basically lived to see this goal realized, and now…what? You may be surprised to find that you have mixed feelings and they aren't all peace and happiness.

Until now, you've been focused on what your ex "should" have been doing, what he should not have been doing, and what he was doing wrong. Perhaps you even kept a journal of these things at your attorney's request. Seeing and staying preoccupied with what "is wrong" with your ex is usually a part of the divorce process. This focus on the failings of your ex may have become almost automatic, and yet it will likely serve as an obstacle if you are now working to successfully move on. Reorienting yourself away from your ex's behavior and onto your own wellbeing after what was likely an exhausting journey will take some work. Divorce tends to bring out the worst in us; our feelings and thoughts can have a profound impact on our behaviors. The process has likely taken its toll, but you can and will experience happiness again despite the changes that have occurred.

Several years ago, a grief counselor (Kubler-Ross & Kessler, 2014) identified five emotions that are often experienced during loss, and some or many of these may occur during the loss of your marriage as well.

Denial.

This can't be happening.
He'll regret this once he sees what it's like when I'm not around.

Anger.

I can't believe that asshole did this to me!
I want to crucify the bastard!

Bargaining.

If only he could see how strapped I am for cash, he wouldn't nickel and dime me so much.
If he understood what this is doing to the kids, maybe things would change.
If we just tried harder, the marriage could survive.

Sadness.

I cry at the drop of a hat.
I never thought I'd be the one getting a divorce.

Acceptance.

I am sad that this ended, but I feel ready to rebuild my life.
Even though this is hard, I know I'll be okay.

As you reach the conclusion of the divorce, you may be surprised to find yourself still feeling stuck in a myriad of emotions. Anger, sadness, relief, and hope may be accompanied by fear, self-doubt, or numbness as well. Many changes have or probably are already occurring in your life, including, perhaps, where you live, your time with your children, your discretionary income, (your non-discretionary income), your friends, and your goals. Acceptance may be your primary goal, but it will likely take time, and it is not uncommon to slip back into anger, sadness, or fear when you encounter things you can't control. Even though the marriage may be officially over, the sting of the emotional and financial consequences of the divorce may feel ever present.

Rachel.
An attractive woman Rachel who had been divorced for over 2 years began dating again. However, she was still plagued by ruminations about her ex who was a physician and had cheated on her during their marriage with a nurse colleague. Following the divorce, the physician married the nurse. Rachel and her ex had 2 children between them during the marriage, both now teenagers. Rachel resented how close her children had grown to the nurse. She blamed her husband's affair for the demise of the marriage itself. She felt alone and betrayed and unable to refocus toward building her own future. Throughout her dates with men she met, the topic of her anger at her ex inevitably entered the conversations, and, not surprisingly, these men stopped contacting her after one or two dates.

Pam.
Another woman Pam was a single mom of two preteens and had been divorced almost 3 years from a wealthy businessman in the community. She had dated only a little since the divorce. Despite their 50-50 time sharing agreement, Pam's ex continued to assume that Pam would be available to take care of their children

when he had work commitments or social activities himself. Since her divorce, she had taken time to build a successful career in the healthcare industry, to engage in yoga and mindful meditation, to improve her diet and physical activity level, to sleep more, and, most importantly, according to Pam, to relish every opportunity to spend quality time with her children. Her finances were limited, and, while she occasionally wished for the resources to provide her children with the fancy clothes, exciting vacations, and summer sports camps that their father was willing and able to provide when they were in his care, she made a commitment to herself to give her children the one gift that she knew she could reliably provide her children: a close, loving, and stable relationship. She generally agreed to provide childcare when her ex was busy, assuming that she had no other commitments. She felt grateful for these extra moments when they came along. Pam was happy when she met her future husband 3 years after her divorce, and she was ready to explore this new and healthy relationship.

I've seen many Rachels and Pams in my work as a psychologist. It may seem random which path an individual will take following a divorce. However, you may be surprised to find that the choices you make as you move forward can have a profound impact on your happiness and quality of life.

Considerations as You Re-emerge from the Cloud of Divorce

Your feelings are neither good nor bad; they are simply information.

While some of your feelings may be painful, allowing yourself to feel your feelings rather than pushing them away or labeling them as good or bad will help you readjust more successfully in the long run. Practice noticing your feelings without judgment as they flow through you, much like you might notice different clouds in the sky. If you find yourself grabbing onto or even trying to control the emotions rather than simply noticing them, simply notice that too and begin again. Feeling your feelings, without judgment, is a process, not a destination.

Build your coping skills.

Prioritize self-care, including physical health, emotional well-being, and social connection. Appendix F includes a self-nourishment checklist that may help you to identify areas of self-care that you are already addressing successfully as well as areas that you might like to improve.

Counseling can be particularly helpful.

If you find that you are struggling to cope with or feel overwhelmed by painful emotions, counseling can be particularly helpful. In addition, if you find yourself turning to unhealthy modes of coping such as excessive drug or alcohol use, talking to someone who understands is a good first step. Appendix D includes information about AA and ALANON. Should painful emotions begin to significantly interfere with your ability to function for more than a few weeks or if you begin to have thoughts of harming yourself or others, talk to someone who can help you to identify sources of support and alternatives to assist you in feeling better. The National Suicide Hot Line is always available at (800) 273-8255; see more information in Appendix C.

Avoid rushing into a new relationship.

This tends to be a greater risk for individuals who are fearful of being alone and who are avoidant of painful emotions. The reality is that healthy relationships depend upon facing the painful emotions and allowing for periods of loneliness.

If you have children, work together with your ex to behave in ways that are in the best interest of the children.

That is, remember to prioritize the well-being of the children and work together to achieve that goal. While you may not feel much like being particularly cooperative with or kind to your ex, remember who this behavior benefits (your children). As the Nike commercials suggest, "Just do it."

Spend a little time finding out who you are and who you would like to be.

Consider what is important to you and make these values your guidepost for making choices. An activity listed in Appendix D is called a Values Card Sort exercise. This is a helpful strategy for identifying what values are most important to you.

Fake it until you make it
(Anonymous AA saying)

You may have decided that you would like to create a new, happy life, but you are unsure if you are ready and how or where to start. There is an old AA saying, "Fake it until you make it," and, it is, in fact, a very good piece of advice. The most effective fix for feeling down, when "your get up and go has got up and went," is to get up and get going anyway. Rather than waiting for life circumstances to improve before making some changes, consider making some changes first. In fact, there's a whole lot of science out there that suggests that the variability in happiness from one person to another has less to do with life circumstances and more to do with our choices to engage in intentional activities that lead to happiness (Lyubomirsky, 2008). Let's explore this a little further.

It may come as a surprise that only 10% of the variability in happiness among individuals is explained by *life circumstances*, such as income, health, education, where you live, and how attractive you are. Only 10%! In fact, people with wealth are only marginally happier than the less wealthy assuming that their basic needs are met. If you think about this, it makes sense. Certainly, lacking the basics for survival can lead to unhappiness, but once these basics are met, having more does not necessarily mean being happier.

In addition, we all tend to be happy initially after a new and pleasant experience, but that feeling quickly dwindles. To experience the happiness high again, we require an additional new and pleasant experience. Scientists call this *hedonic adaptation*, and from a physical health standpoint, it serves a purpose. I like to refer to hedonic adaptation as the *Lego Effect*. When my son was younger, he loved Legos. Actually, what he loved were new Legos in a *brand-new box*. Whenever he was given a new Lego set, I got into the habit of timing him to see how long he would remain happily engrossed with the new Legos. He was a speedy little assembler, and I wanted to make sure that we were getting our money's worth. What I quickly realized was that the amount of time he enjoyed his Lego set was related to the amount of time that it took to assemble the pieces in the set. The cost of the set was related to the number of pieces and the difficulty of the set. With some basic math, I was able to see approximately how much one minute of Lego enjoyment cost (and, by the way, it wasn't cheap)! Once the set was assembled and the newness of the set wore off, the Legos lost their power to keep him happy and entertained, and he began to wish for a new and "even better" set. This decrease in pleasure over time was that Lego Effect.

Most thrilling life circumstances, such as that increase in pay, fancy car, or new and bigger house have a similar effect on our happiness, a transient one that diminishes as the newness wears off.

So then, if life circumstances only account for 10% of the variation in happiness, what explains the other 90%? There are many other factors that influence how happy we are. Each of us does, in fact, have a relative *set point* of happiness. That is, some people are just born happier than others. 50% of the variability in happiness among individuals is driven by this *heritability* factor. This is essentially the baseline level of happiness that you are born with, and, since you can't change your genetics, it is what it is, relatively speaking.

Happiness is a butterfly which, when pursued, is always beyond our grasp,
but, if you will sit down quietly, may alight upon you (Anonymous)

So far, we have only accounted for 60% of the variability in happiness within people. But what about the final 40%? Can we influence this remaining 40% and perhaps increase our level of happiness? The short answer is "yes!" The remaining 40% of the variability in happiness is influenced by the intentional activities that we choose to engage in. Intentional activities are those that are associated with people and experiences rather than physical possessions. Simply put, we have the best chance for increasing our own level of happiness if we regularly engage in intentional activities.

There are a variety of intentional activities that have been shown to influence happiness, including being mindful, engaging in behaviors rooted in your values, identifying things that you are grateful for, sharing through acts of kindness, and expanding your empathy. The benefits to increased levels of happiness do not stop with the positive feeling itself. Studies have shown that greater happiness is associated with greater work productivity and work quality, more satisfying relationships, higher energy, a stronger immune system and better heart health, decreased stress levels, reduced pain, and a longer life.

Committing to rebuilding your life and finding happiness is a big step. Breaking it down into smaller, more manageable goals can help you get started. At the end of this book in Appendix D there are additional resources that you may find helpful in your journey. These resources include a self-nourishment checklist, a link to a free 8-week online Happiness course, and a link to an inspiring Ted talk entitled "The Happy Secret to Better Work." Following the appendices in this book is a reference list that includes references to several books and articles on happiness, acceptance and commitment, mindfulness, and healthy relationships.

A final note from Dr. Jenkins.

You have embarked on this journey, you've collected a great deal of useful information, and, whether you are at the beginning or the end of your divorce, you've decided to take that next step. If I had a magic wand, I would wish for you to know the following things. You are a good person. You have learned a great deal from your experiences. Don't let go of your positive memories; holding tightly onto these memories does not make your decision to move on a mistake. It's okay to feel loss. It's okay to feel afraid. These feelings will pass. Notice your anger, but don't hang on to it; If you attach to your anger, it will steal your joy. Acceptance is your goal. You have wonderful experiences awaiting you. They are out there, just around the corner.   *-Beth*

13

Issues After Divorce

Second time around.
As I stated in the introduction, for about 18 years I owned the largest bridal store in Florida. One Saturday a woman in her late 70's approached me and asked if I was the owner. When I said "yes" she stated that she had an important question to ask. She went on to say that she had been married for almost 40 years, but that for the last 8 years she had been a widow. Then she looked me in the eye and said, "You know I have not had relations with a man in 8 years." Wondering to myself why I needed to know this, I asked how I could be of assistance. She continued, stating that she had been married by a magistrate the first time and had never worn a wedding gown. She had always wanted to wear one and now that she was getting married again, she wanted to know if it was okay if she wore white. Without missing a beat I looked her in the eye and said, "Ma'am, the statute of limitations is 7 years, so, since you have not had relations with a man for 8, you are absolutely permitted to wear a white wedding gown." She smiled from ear to ear and went on to buy a full princess style gown with a royal cathedral train.

Post-Divorce Housekeeping Details

First, be sure to follow up with the legal details like getting a quit-claim deed recorded if you are getting the house. If your final agreement provided that your husband name you as a beneficiary on a life insurance policy (to make sure child support or alimony is covered if he dies), have your attorney send a copy of the agreement to the insurance company requesting that they notify you if coverage is changed or the policy is dropped for non-payment, etc.

My suggestion is that when your divorce is totally final, make another appointment with your divorce attorney to develop a check list of all the housekeeping details that should be done.

Common Problems Post-Divorce

Most divorces will end with you and your husband signing some form of property settlement agreement as well as a custody or parenting agreement if you have minor children. In most states these agreements will then be incorporated as a court order. This means that the agreements are more than just contracts that would require a separate lawsuit to enforce them. Instead, these agreements are now court orders and the failure to abide and comply with the terms can be enforced as a contempt of court proceeding. When you have that post-divorce meeting with your lawyer to do the housekeeping details, be sure to ask if in your state the final divorce made your agreements a court order.

In most states, a contempt of court finding, besides making the ex-spouse comply, can carry additional fines, legal fees and even jail sentences in some cases.

Post-Divorce Obligations

Child Support.

The amount of child support can be adjusted up or down. Some states require that you prove a change in circumstances like a parent's income increase or decrease and other states only require that the amount being paid no longer fall within their guidelines in order for a change or modification in child support to occur. If payments are not being made or received, be sure to talk to your attorney about the enforcement methods available in your state. Child support obligations generally end when the child turns 18 or is out of high school, whichever occurs last, but here again review this with your attorney. It is also important to note that in many states the amount being paid for 2 children does not get cut in half when support for the older child ends. I have seen many cases where the support went from about 30% of the payer's income for 2 children to 20% of the payer's income for one child. Your attorney should be able to access your state's guidelines to give you an idea of how much you should be getting and how much it will change when there is no longer an obligation for a child who turns 18 and is out of school.

Support for higher education or college is generally not required of a parent unless it has been provided for in the property settlement agreement.

Alimony.

This is a support payment made by one spouse to the other for the benefit of the spouse and not children. The ability to change or modify the amount will be determined by the language you agreed to in your property settlement. Some people have set up non-modifiable alimony except under certain circumstances in their agreements, while others will have agreements allowing for modifications based on changed circumstances like an income change for one of the parties.

With alimony that resulted from a court determination by the judge, the amounts being paid are generally modifiable when there is a change in circumstances. Your attorney should be able to explain to you when and under what circumstances the alimony can be changed.

Alimony is often for a set period of time and this is something that should also be discussed with your attorney. Also review the tax obligations regarding alimony with your attorney as this is a changing area of law.

Life and health insurance requirements.

Often the property settlement agreement will include a provision requiring the paying spouse to have life insurance naming the other spouse as a beneficiary. The amount required for this life insurance is often the amount needed to replace the support and/or alimony obligation in the event of the payor's death. The agreement should also have a provision requiring the payor to provide yearly proof of the insurance policy.

Your state's support laws and your final property settlement agreement may also have provisions relating to who is responsible for paying health insurance premiums for the benefit of a spouse and the children of the marriage. These are important areas to discuss with your attorney during settlement discussions and at your post-divorce conference.

Debt obligations.

As previously stated, your settlement will have divided the debts of the marriage as well as the assets. Often the obligations relating to debts will go beyond the final divorce date, so this is an area that you should be discussing with your attorney at your post-divorce conference.

If your husband agreed to assume and pay off certain debts, be sure to follow up and request verification. Finally, it is important to make sure all joint credit card accounts are canceled so that your husband does not incur new debt that could affect your credit.

Update estate planning and pension beneficiaries.

Creating a will, if you don't have one, or updating you will, if you do have one, is in order once your divorce is final (or even sooner). This is something important to review with your attorney. Additionally, if you are to receive part of your husband's pension, follow up with your attorney and CPA to make sure a Qualified Domestic Relations Order is put in place and sent to the pension manager. With respect to your pensions, be sure to change the beneficiary designation if it is a pension that pays anything after your death. Also, be sure to review your life insurance policies to change the beneficiaries where it's appropriate.

Changing your name.

Many states make it easy to re-take your maiden name or completely change your name after a divorce. Often the post-divorce name change process is far easier than the process to change your name absent a divorce. If this is something you may be interested in doing, be sure to discuss this with your attorney before the divorce is final as in many states it can be accomplished at the same time the final divorce decree is issued.

Epilogue

Note: I would suggest that you wait to read these last thoughts until your divorce is final.

As I mentioned in the introduction to this book, my initial inspiration for "Crucify the Bastard" came about because I met so many women in social settings who, upon learning that I was a divorce attorney, would share with me the reasons they were personally dissatisfied with how their divorce had turned out. In most of these cases, I would think to myself that if only the woman had picked a better attorney or had been a little better educated about the process, she would not have had the problems she described.

What I also noticed was that many of these women had not fully moved on with their lives and too many still carried some wounds, resentment, or even outright anger, that stemmed from their former marriages and the experience of getting divorced. These feelings and emotions clearly were impeding their ability to totally move on to new, rewarding relationships and adventures.

Fortunately, I have also met many women who have found that their new lives are so much better and happier than the ones they left behind. These were the women who were able to let go of their anger and, instead, hold onto the memories from their prior marriage that were joyful and fun. They shifted from blaming their former husbands as being solely responsible for the failure of the marriage to recognizing and focusing on their own contribution to the success or failure of relationships, which better prepared them for future, healthy relationships.

Even when these women had married men who were physically or emotionally abusive and escape/separation was imperative, many recognized that warning signs may have been present prior to their marriages, and they expressed determination to recognize such warning signs in future relationships.

So, my parting advice is for you to remember that you alone must be responsible for your own happiness. You must let go of the anger and instead reframe the negative experiences from your former marriage as learning experiences. Recognize that if there was infidelity by either you or your husband, this was simply a symptom of a bigger problem in the marriage and not the cause of your divorce. Recognize that even if you felt that the divorce result was unfair to you or that you were victimized, being angry or resentful about it now is not going to change the past. We all know that often life is not fair, but what we should all also remember is that keeping and nurturing anger and resentment will only poison and sabotage your ability to move on and find happiness, fulfilling relationships, and joyous adventures. Accept your past experiences for what they were, and, perhaps, with a little gratitude, since the knowledge you gained from your past has made you a wiser and better person today.

Appendix A
General Marital Summary Sheet

This is a list of general information to be provided in advance to attorneys you are considering hiring. I suggest that you email this information to the attorney prior to your appointment. If you are not comfortable sharing this information in advance, I suggest printing it out to hand to the attorney at the start of the appointment.

1. Your current address, phone number, email address, how long have you been at this residence.

2. Your age / Date of birth (DOB), your spouse's age (DOB).

3. Length of marriage. Date of marriage. Date of separation (if applicable).

4. Number of children of this marriage. Age and date of birth of each child.

5. Your approximate income from all sources (per month or year). Your spouse's approximate income from all sources (per month or year).

6. List the name of your current employer and the length of time you have worked for them. If less than five years provide the names of all prior employers covering at least your last five years. Do the same for your spouse.

7. Are you still living under the same roof as your spouse (in the same household)? If not, who moved out and where is the other spouse living and how long has he lived there?

8. Do you and your spouse own a home? Approximate/rough value of the marital home. Approximate/rough amount owed on the marital home for all mortgages.

9. Do you or your spouse own any other real estate (jointly or separately)? If yes, list the address of said real estate, approximate/rough value, and list the amount owed on any loans/mortgages on said real estate.

10. Approximate/rough value of all financial accounts including

checking/savings accounts, stock and/or investment accounts. List whose name said accounts are in.

11. Do you or your spouse have any pensions or retirement IRA accounts? State whose name the retirement accounts are in and the estimated value if you know it.

12. Provide an estimated amount of all debt for both you and your spouse that does not include mortgages (credit cards, personal loans, etc.).

13. Reason for needing to see a divorce attorney. Provide a short summary of your major reasons that you are considering filing for a divorce. If your spouse has already filed for divorce provide a short summary of any marital misconduct or other problems (drug or alcohol abuse, physical abuse, adultery, etc.)

Appendix B
Questions for Potential Lawyers

1. What percentage of your work involves divorce?

2. How long have you been practicing law? Can you tell me a little about yourself?

3. Do you know my spouse? Do you know my spouse's attorney?

4. Do you know how many of the local judges deal with divorces? Can you give me a summary of your experience with each of them? Do you feel you know what their biases are?

5. Have you had any experience with finding hidden assets? How have you done this?

6. Have you had experience dealing with custody where the other parents problems are _____, _____, and _____.

7. Can you tell me the steps and procedures my case will follow?

8. Can you tell me what parts of my case you will personally handle and what parts others in your firm will handle? Can I meet those others?

9. Will I receive a copy of all correspondence and legal documents in my case?

10. Will you be doing monthly updates and summaries as to what is going on in my case that can be sent to me?

11. What is your retainer; what happens if all the retainer is not used; what is your hourly rate?

12. With respect to custody can you give me your impression as to the likely result in my case?

13. With respect to child support can you give me a rough idea as to what the guidelines show I would get?

14. With respect to spousal support or alimony can you give me an idea as to the procedure and the probability of getting it and how much I would get? What factors are used to determine getting spousal support or alimony?

15. What are the possibilities of getting my spouse to pay my attorney fees and court costs?

16. How often will I receive a summary of how my retainer is being used?

17. How long do you take to return a phone call or answer an email? Is there a way to reach you in an emergency? How would you define an emergency?

18. Do you have a problem with me trying to negotiate directly with my spouse after we have full disclosure of all the assets and debts? Would you help prep me for this by telling me the likely outcome?

19. Based on everything I've shared, how would you predict a judge would rule on the different aspects of my case?

Appendix C
What to Bring to Your First
Meeting with a Lawyer

Note: Do not worry at this point about being completely accurate or complete with the asset and debt information. Your lawyer will have the ability to search for assets, get appraisals, and get bank statements, etc. At the initial interview, your lawyer just needs to have a general idea as to what the value of the marital estate is.

1. General Marital Summary Sheet if you have not already sent it to the attorney prior to your meeting (see Appendix A). If your spouse has already filed for divorce, bring copies of all documents you have received.

2. Asset summary sheet. To the best of your abilities make a list of all the things you and/or your husband own but do not include furniture or possessions unless they are very valuable like antiques or collectables. Remember, you do not have to have the exact values, your best guess is all you need at this point (your lawyer can get the exact values later).

    a. List all assets that you or your husband had before the marriage that existed on the date you got married. Include real estate, financial accounts, retirement accounts, etc. Use your best guess to assign a value to each. List what happened to each of these assets during the marriage.

    b. List of all homes and real estate.

i. State who is listed on the deed as the owner and be sure to include real estate owned by your husband, even if your name is not on it.

ii. For each one, list your best guess as to the total value and then list, to the best of your ability, the approximate debt or the amount that is owed in the form of a mortgage or other debt, and list who or what bank or finance company has the loan.

iii. For each home or real estate parcel, list the approximate date of when it was acquired.

iv. If there was any money put down on the home or real estate, state where that money came from (example: savings, gift from a parent, etc.).

v. If either you or your husband owned a home or any real estate before the marriage, list it and if it was sold state approximately when and what happened to any money that was gained for the sale.

vi. List all financial assets that you believe exist like bank accounts, savings accounts, stock accounts, retirement accounts, pensions, etc. Include the name of the bank or financial institution and list the approximate value of each account.

vii. List any inheritances that either you or your husband received before or during the marriage and the approximate value. Also state what happened to the inheritance (example: "used to buy another home" or "still in husband's name," etc.).

3. Debt summary sheet.
   a. All loans and the approximate amount owed and what the money was used for. State if there is any collateral. (example: car loans, home mortgages, home equity loans, personal loans to family members or friends). For each loan, list the approximate monthly payment and state the name of the person who has been paying the loan and the source of the funds they use to make the payment.

   b. All credit card debt. List the name of the credit card, the name of the person who has the card, the total amount owed on the credit card, and what the card debt was used for. For each credit card debt, list the approximate monthly payment and state the name of the person who has been paying the loan and the source of the funds they use to make the payment.

4. List of valuable personal possessions. For each item or group, list your best estimate or guess as to the value. Also list who has possession of the item and if the item(s) were acquired before or during the marriage (example: antique furniture, coin collections, collections, etc.).

Appendix D
Online Resources

Safety Resources:

National Suicide Prevention Lifeline (800) 273-8255
➤ http://www.suicidepreventionlifeline.org/
The National Domestic Violence Hotline
➤ http://www.thehotline.org/resources/victims-and-survivors/
Additional Domestic Violence Resources
➤ https://www.helpguide.org/articles/abuse/domestic-violence-and-abuse.htm
➤ http://domesticviolence.org/personalized-safety-plan/
➤ http://www.thehotline.org/help/path-to-safety/

Substance Abuse Resources:

Alcoholics Anonymous
➤ http://www.aa.org/
Narcotics Anonymous
➤ http://www.na.org/
Al-Anon
➤ http://www.al-anon.org/

Mental Health and Happiness:

Ted Talk- Shawn Achor: The Happy Secret to Better Work
➤ https://www.ted.com/
Values Card Sort
➤ Cards: http://www.motivationalinterviewing.org/sites/default/files/valuescardsort_0.pdf
➤ Instructions:

https://motivationalinterviewing.org/sites/defa
ult/files/valuesinstructions.pdf
Free Eight Week Course on Happiness
  ➢ http://www.thehotline.org/resources/victims-
    and-survivors/
Free Online Mindfulness-Based Stress Reduction
Course
  ➢ http://www.palousemindfulness.com/

Online Mindfulness Meditation and Sleep Apps:

  • Calm
  • Insight Timer
  • VA Administration CBT-i Coach for
    Insomnia

Appendix E
Duluth Model of Power and Control

DOMESTIC ABUSE INTERVENTION PROGRAMS
202 East Superior Street
Duluth, Minnesota 55802
218-722-2781
www.theduluthmodel.org

From "The Duluth Model Power and Control Wheel," by the Domestic Abuse Intervention Project, (Retrieved from http://theduluthmodel.org). Reprinted with permission.

Appendix F
Jenkins Self-Care Checklist

According to the World Health Organization, health "is a state of complete physical, mental, and social well-being, and not merely the absence of disease or infirmity." Your mind and your body are connected. The following self-care checklist can help you identify areas for improvement in your life. Engaging in these activities not only increases mental well-being and decreases the likelihood of depression or anxiety, it also supports improved physical and interpersonal health. As you review the list, note the activities that you are already doing well. Then you may want to mark the areas that you would like to devote more time and attention to as you move forward. You may also decide to add additional items to this list.

Physical Nourishment

Sleep. Good sleep leads to good memory and good health. To determine how much sleep you need per night, note the amount that helps you to feel your best during the day. For some this is 8 hours, and for others, it may be more or less.

Healthy Eating. A healthy plate includes ¼ carbs, ¼ protein and ½ vegetables and fruit. Three meals per day with 1-2 healthy snacks maintain a stable blood sugar and give you the energy you need to get through the day.

Drinking plenty of water. We are made up of 50-75% water. Life depends on us keeping it that way. The minimum amount of water a person should try to drink per day is 9-13 cups. Caffeine and alcohol work against your goal of being well-hydrated. When you fail to drink enough water, you are likely to have less energy and feel easily fatigued.

Physical Activity. Physical activity includes exercise and movement. Regularly engaging in movement is important for good health. Monitoring physical activity levels with a watch or smart phone can often help you to stay on track.

Preventive Health Care. Preventive health care includes scheduling your annual visits to your primary care provider, staying up to date with preventive vaccines, regular dental care, and engaging in positive health behaviors such as hand washing, good sleep hygiene, physical activity, healthy eating, smoking cessation, and limiting alcohol consumption.

Unplug. We have heard it a million times. Take time to unplug from the tv, the phone, and the computer.

Grooming. Taking care of your body reminds you that you are a valuable individual. Stay clean. Keep your nails manicured. Get regular haircuts. Shave.

Temperature. Keeping your surroundings at a comfortable temperature can improve mental alertness and mood during the day and quality of sleep at night.

Physical Touch. Physical touch is essential to good health. Hug your kids. Love your furry friends. Get a massage.

Comfortable clothing. Wear clothes you like. Choose soft fabrics and comfortable shoes. Avoid tight fitting clothes.

Relaxation. Yoga, progressive muscle relaxation, and tai chi are three of many physical activities that can lead to both physical relaxation as well as a mental sense of calm and acceptance.

Create your space. Find your space and make it your own. It doesn't need to be a large space. Keep the space inviting, safe, and comfortable. Remember that your surroundings often represent your insides; chaos outside reflects chaos on the inside. Organizing your space will increase your sense of control. Having a comfortable living space reduces anxiety and stress.

Emotional Nourishment

Have fun. Seek out activities that you enjoy. Schedule them into your day. Refill.

Seek creativity and learning. Find something new to learn or do. Engage your creative side. Finding a creative activity that you enjoy doing can help you find flow, a state of being highly focused and "in the zone." Flow has been shown to increase happiness.

Practice gratitude. Notice and appreciate the large and small things in your daily life. At the end of each day, you may choose to recall 3 new things that you are grateful for. This simple exercise has been shown to increase happiness.

Finding meaning and purpose. Examine and prioritize your values and create goals that reflect who you are and who you would like to be. Complete a values identification exercise. There are many available for free online, for example, www.motivationalinterviewing.org/sites/default/files/value scardsort_0.pdf

Set limits. Practice assertive communication versus aggressive, passive, or passive-aggressive communication. Describe the problem, ask about and listen to the other person's experience or behavior, assert your needs, and negotiate a win-win solution. Practice saying "no" to things you don't want to do.

Practice mindfulness. Practice paying attention to something, on purpose, without judgment. Making this activity a regular habit comes with all sorts of health benefits.

Notice inner experiences. Take time each morning and evening to take your "emotional pulse" and tune in to what you are feeling. Consider and challenge your thoughts, beliefs, judgments, and assumptions.

Appreciate nature. Take a walk outside. Pay attention to the world around you: the sounds, smells, and sights. It doesn't cost a thing!

Affirm your own value. Notice what you are doing well and how you might do things even better yet. This subtle shift from looking backward to looking forward can do wonders for your outlook.

Social Support

Stay connected. Appreciate your family supports. Make time for friends. Ask for and accept help. Give support to others.

Groups. Make time for group interactions such as sports, creative activities, and spiritual activities.

Community. Connect with others through community action, spiritual activities, volunteer work, school activities, or neighborhood associations.

Volunteer to help others. Giving back brings a sense of value and purpose.

Add Your Own Ideas for Self-Care

References

Anonymous (1957-1960). When your get up and go has got up and went. *The Globe-Democrat.*

Boehm, J. K., Peterson, C., Kivimaki, M., & Kubzansky, L. D. (2011). Heart health when life is satisfying: evidence from the Whitehall II cohort study. *European Heart Journal,* 32(21) 2672-2677.

Brockis, J. (2019). Why Happiness at Work Matters. Retrieved from: https://www.drjennybrockis.com/2019/1/24/happiness-work-matters/

Chida, Y. & Steptoe, A. (2008). Positive psychological well-being and mortality: a quantitative review of prospective observational studies. *Psychosomatic Medicine,* 70(7), 741-756.

Cohen, S., Doyle, W. J., Turner, R. B., Alper, C. M., & Skoner, D. P. (2003). Emotional style and susceptibility to the common cold. *Psychosomatic Medicine,* 65(4), 652-657.

Davidson, K., Mostofsky, M., & Whang, W. (2010). Don't worry, be happy: positive affect and reduced 10-year incident coronary heart disease: The Canadian Nova Scotia Health Survey. *European Heart Journal,* 31(9), 1065-1070.

Doskow, E. (2016). Nolo's essential guide to divorce. Bang Printing.

The Duluth Model Power and Control Wheel. (1981). The Domestic Abuse Intervention Project. Retrieved from http://theduluthmodel.org

Emmons, R. A. & McCullough, M. E. (2003). Counting blessings versus burdens: An experimental investigation of gratitude and subjective well-being in daily life. *Journal of Personality and Social Psychology,* 84(2), 377-389.

Fredrickson, B. (2004). The broaden-and-build theory of positive emotions. *Philosophical Transactions of the Royal Society of London.* Series B: Biological Sciences, 359(1449), 1367-1377.

Gallup (2007). The State of the American Workplace. Retrieved from https://news.gallup.com/reports/199961/7.asp

Gottman, J. M. & Silver, N. (1995). Why marriages succeed or fail: And how you can make yours last. Simon & Schuster - New York.

Headon, T., Jones, M., Simonon, P., & Strummer, J. (1981). Should I Stay or Should I Go [Recorded by The Clash]. On *Combat Rock* [Record]. CBS. (1982).

Hickson, W. E. (1984). Perseverance; Or Try Again. In Hickson, W. E., Bernarr, R., & Hewitt, L., *The Singing Master: (1836), Volume 10 of Classic texts in music education.* Boethius Press, 1984.

Kubler-Ross, E., & Kessler, D. (2014). Finding the meaning of grief through the five stages of loss. *On Grief and Grieving.* London: Simon & Schuster.

L. (1948, June 23). A chapter of definitions. *The Daily Crescent*, 2, Column 4.

Lawrence, E. M., Rogers, R. G., & Wadsworth, T. (2015). Happiness and longevity in the United States. *Social Science & Medicine* (1982), 145,115-119.

Lyubomirsky, S. (2008). The how of happiness: A scientific approach to getting the life you want. New York, NY: Penguin Press.

Lyubomirsky, S. (2011) Hedonic adaptation to positive and negative experiences. In Folkman, S. (Ed.), Oxford handbook of stress, health, and coping, 200-224, New York, NY: Oxford University Press.

Schlitz, D. (1976). The Gambler [Recorded by Kenny Rogers]. On *The Gambler* [Record]. United Artists. (1978).

Sgroi, D. (2015). Happiness and Productivity: Understanding the Happy Productive Worker. SMF-CAGE Global Perspective Series.

Steptoe, A., O'Donnell, K., Marmot, M., & Wardle, J. (2008). Positive affect, psychological well-being, and good sleep. *Journal of Psychosomatic Research*, 64(4), 409-415.

Stone, A. A., Cox, D. S., Valdimarsdottier, H., Jandorf, L., & Neale, J. M. (1987). Evidence that secretory IgA antibody is associated with daily mood. *Journal of Personality and Social*

Psychology, 52(5), 988-993.

Strand, E. B., Zautra, A. J., Thoresen, M., Ødegård, S., Uhlig, T., & Finset, A. (2006). Positive affect as a factor of resilience in the pain-negative affect relationship in patients with rheumatoid arthritis. *Journal of Psychosomatic Research*, 60(5), 477-484.

Zautra, A. J., Johnson, L. M., & Davis, M. C. (2005). Positive affect as a source of resilience for women in chronic pain. *Journal of Consulting and Clinical Psychology*, 73(2), 212-220.

ABOUT THE AUTHORS

Jon M. Saltzman, Esq.   **www.CrucifytheBastard.com**

Jon M. Saltzman, Esq., is the founding partner of the law firm of Saltzman and Gordon in Allentown, PA. The firm specializes in family law, limiting their practice to divorce, custody, and child and spousal support. Jon opened the firm in 1985; today he is semi-retired and is of-counsel to the firm. He is admitted to practice law before the Supreme Court of PA, The Federal District Courts for the Eastern District of PA, and the Northern District of CA. He is also admitted to the 3rd and 9th Federal Circuit Courts of Appeal.

In retirement, Jon opened Jon's Bridal, which was the largest bridal store in Florida. When asked about the reason for the switch, he said, "I was ready to see women who walked in the door happy for a change."

Jon had been married for 29 years when he and his wife Robin mutually decided to divorce. Owning businesses and real estate, the marital assets were somewhat complex. After her initial consultation with a divorce lawyer, Robin announced to Jon, "I've decided who I want to be my divorce lawyer…you." She added, "I just know you, and, if I hire anyone else, you will eat them alive. I also know that, if you are my lawyer, you will be fair and bend over backwards to take care of me [your client], and I will come out just fine." Jon agreed, prepared a property settlement agreement, and insisted that Robin take it to an independent divorce lawyer before signing it. She did and reported back that her lawyer advised her that the agreement was "more than fair." Jon and Robin remain friends today.

Elizabeth A. Jenkins, PhD   **www.EvenBetterYet.com**

Co-author Dr. Elizabeth Jenkins is the developing owner of Professional Health Consulting and co-developer of MI-Lead (Motivational Interviewing for Leadership). She is a licensed clinical psychologist, published author, and public speaker providing coaching and counseling with professionals to address behavior change, leadership development, communication skills building, and distress management. She has successfully completed Florida Supreme Court approved family mediation certification training as well as Florida approved parenting coordination training. Dr. Jenkins is a Courtesy Assistant Professor of Psychiatry and Behavioral Medicine at the University of South Florida, and she has over 20 years of experience serving in the Veteran's Health Administration. She has been a clinician for the NFL's Success Without Substances Program since 2010, and, for over 15 years, she has provided continuing education and training addressing disruptive behavior in physicians.

Made in the USA
Middletown, DE
07 January 2021